IMAGES OF ENGLAND

EXETER
POSTCARDS

This book belongs to

N. PERCY

HIGH STREET.

OLD EXE BRIDGE.

JUBILEE CLOCK TOWER.

MOL'S COFFEE HOUSE.

THE GUILDHALL.

THE CATHEDRAL.

ALBERT MEMORIAL MUSEUM.

HOTEL

CATHEDRAL FROM EAST.

CATHEDRAL CHOIR.

ROUGEMONT CASTLE.

Exeter.

IMAGES OF ENGLAND

EXETER
POSTCARDS

JOHN AND MARGARET FOLKES

TEMPUS

Frontispiece: Exeter in postcards, on a postcard of early 1905. Long-established places of interest for a visitor to the city which are still largely unchanged in 2005, such as the Cathedral, Rougemont Castle, Mol's Coffee House and the Jubilee Clock Tower, are portrayed on the miniature cards illustrated together with other images of Exeter before the dramatic changes which occurred later in that year. The 1778 stone bridge, then undergoing demolition, is already described as the 'Old Stone Bridge', while High Street, the Guildhall, Queen Street and the Royal Albert Memorial Museum are seen before the advent of trams and, later on, cars.

First published 2005

Tempus Publishing Limited
The Mill, Brimscombe Port,
Stroud, Gloucestershire, GL5 2QG
www.tempus-publishing.com

British Library Cataloguing in Publication Data.
A catalogue record for this book is available from the British Library.

ISBN 0 7524 3474 8

Typesetting and origination by Tempus Publishing Limited.
Printed in Great Britain.

Contents

Acknowledgements 6

Introduction 7

one Views for the Visitor 9

two Shops and Shopping 33

three Events, Entertainment and Sport 53

four Education 69

five City in Crisis 81

six Outside the Walls 97

seven The Eventful Year of 1905 115

Acknowledgements

Special thanks are due to present and past members of the Exeter Postcard Society, now celebrating its twentieth year, who have allowed us to include postcards from their collections or who have contributed advice and personal recollections from their life in Exeter. In particular we should mention Lynda Pearce, Don Lashbrook, Christine Trigger, Mavis Piller and Ed Mills. Thanks are also due to Gill Walsh and Tony Davison, who loaned us cards, and to Jacqueline Cummins for her specialised local knowledge.

We are grateful to the Isca Collection for allowing us to use images for which they hold the copyright.

We very much appreciated the help and advice given by Roger Brien and James Turner of the Devon and Exeter Institution and the staff of the West Country Studies Library.

We also thank our editor at Tempus Publishing, Matilda Pearce, for her ongoing patience, friendliness and guidance.

Much of the supporting textual information included has been gained from detailed study of contemporary printed and manuscript material, but over sixty books have also been consulted as part of our research.

We have made every endeavour to track down the owners of the copyright for all images used and apologise to anyone not mentioned.

Introduction

At the commencement of the twentieth century, Exeter was still in touch with the roots of its surrounding countryside. Many of today's suburbs were villages or at most small towns, and although many majestic buildings adorned Exeter's streets, its shops were still individually owned and personal service was always preferred to impersonal mass marketing. No mechanical transport polluted the atmosphere at ground level and no aeroplanes roared, or even spluttered, in the skies above. Queen Victoria still reigned in the twilight of the nineteenth century, but Britain was at war, fighting the Boers.

The next sixty years saw remarkable changes as gramophones were replaced by radio, and magic lanterns eventually by television. Exonians endured four wars (the Boer War, First World War, Second World War and the Korean War) and suffered heavy losses in both World Wars. In the First World War, many young men marched off to battle optimistically, only to meet their deaths in the trenches. In the Second World War, the conflict came to Exeter itself in a series of air raids, culminating in the devastating Blitz of May 1942. At a pivotal point in Exeter's history, much of the fabric and elegance of the city's architecture was swept aside by bomb blast and fire, never to be replaced, and many of its citizens were wounded or killed.

In an age when few people owned telephones and before the advent of radio and television, national and local newspapers were the main source of information on current affairs. Local newspapers, in addition to national and international news, provided immense detail on local events and personalities but without the photographs that should logically have accompanied them. When the cinema was in its infancy and cameras were only owned by the few who could afford them, for many the only visual record available was the postcard. Although accepted by the Post Office in 1894, British postcards were initially smaller than their continental cousins, with the sender's message and a small picture forced to compete for space on the front. However, in 1902 the message space was moved onto the back of the card beside the address, and as pictures now filled the entire front of the cards, the golden age of the picture postcard had begun.

Local photographers seized the opportunity to photograph every imaginable subject, from local places of interest to events ranging from weddings and funerals to accidents, fires and even the first ever sighting in the area of an aeroplane in flight and on the ground. Picture postcards brought an immediacy to events, as a visual record of any event could be available to be sent to relatives and friends across Britain for only a half-penny (half the price of letter post) in only a few hours. Others recorded scenes of everyday life that could be preserved in albums for posterity. Postcard publishers multiplied as the rapid growth of this versatile new visual medium presented a new marketing opportunity, and cards were sold direct from publishers or from outlets such as tobacconists, stationers and post offices. Because of the wide availability of these inexpensive cards, a new collecting craze grew rapidly and every possible subject (from street views and theatres to piers and paddle steamers) was covered and collected. Floods of comic cards came from specialist publishers and the demand for designs was enormous.

By 1909, over 860 million cards had passed through the post and traffic was still expanding. During the First World War propaganda cards proliferated, but cards from foreign (and especially German) publishers, which had previously dominated the postcard scene, disappeared. In June 1918 the postage rate for a postcard doubled. Coupled with the spread of the private telephone, greater mobility provided by the growth in the ownership of cars and the increased number of photographs reproduced in newspapers, the number and quality of cards declined, although there was a partial revival during the Second World War. The popularity of collecting postcards also diminished, but since the 1970s, supported by an ever-increasing numbers of books, magazines, collectors fairs and exhibitions, it has revived, and it is now one of the top three collecting hobbies in the country.

Using contemporary material, from newspapers and other sources in the first six decades of the twentieth century, combined with over 200 archive postcards selected from the collections of members of the Exeter Postcard Society (now celebrating its twentieth year), this book looks in detail at the events behind the visual images to recreate moments of excitement, enjoyment, humour, anxiety and sudden death in a period of the city's past which is on the cusp of history and memory.

Subjects explored in depth include buildings and areas that were favourite destinations for the tourist, many of which still remain, and some of those which were lost to enemy action during the Second World War, as well as the many changes that took place in shops and shopping. Momentous events are examined, including the Great Air Race of 1911 and the proclamation of George V's accession to the throne in the preceding year. Entertainment and sport sections cover theatres, cinemas and restaurants, together with Exeter's football, rugby and cricket teams. Other chapters trace the expansion of education in the city, from primary schools to colleges and the establishment of Exeter University, and the stories behind the dramatic images of accidents, fires, floods and war. Early postcards graphically demonstrate the changes that have occurred in the small villages, towns and areas surrounding Exeter which are now integral suburbs of the city.

An entire chapter is devoted to the events of 1905, when Exeter acquired a new bridge, a new electric tram service, a new statue and a new sense of civic pride during the momentous mayoralty of Councillor Edwin C. Perry.

John and Margaret Folkes
January 2005

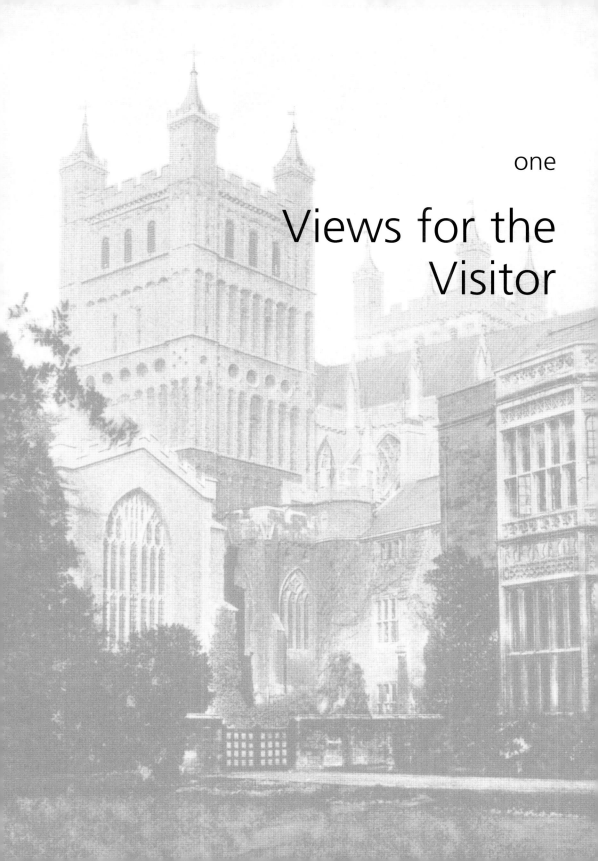

one

Views for the Visitor

South Tower, Exeter Cathedral

The South Tower of Exeter Cathedral, early in the twentieth century. The Norman tower holds the heaviest peal of bells in England, including the massive tenor bell Grandisson, cast in 1729 and recast in 1902, which weighs 72½ cwt. At the time of this picture the thirteen bells had a total weight of 13 tons 11¾cwt. The peal is now even heavier: in 1979 a new bell, Jubilee, was added which weighs 5¾ cwt. Bellringers in the past supposedly had to observe a strict set of rules, which were displayed on the wall of the belfry. Failure to observe them was punished with a monetary forfeit. The eclectic rules included: 'Whoever comes to the Tower disguised in liquor shall forfeit 6d' and 'Whoever reads these Articles with their Hat on their head shall forfeit 6d'. The worst fine of 1 shilling was imposed on 'Whoever Fights or offers to Fight'!

Exeter Cathedral, west front. This card shows the eighteenth century great west window undergoing restoration and refilling. Work was completed on 1 July 1904, two days before this card was posted. The restored window, dedicated to the late Archbishop of Canterbury, Frederick Temple, was unveiled in the presence of a large gathering of dignitaries, including his widow. The window was destroyed in the Blitz of 1942, but was restored in memory of William Temple, Frederick's son and also Archbishop of Canterbury (from 1942-1944), who was born in Exeter.

The west front of Exeter Cathedral in 1905, published by the Paris-based publisher Louis Levy, who also had an office in London. The medieval Image Screen is beautifully carved in Beer stone, in three tiers: the top shows apostles, prophets and saints; the second shows kings, bishops and crusaders; and the bottom shows angels. Recent research of paint samples on the statues revealed that the entire screen was once brightly coloured.

Left: Old clock on the wall of the north transept of Exeter Cathedral in 1905. Parts of this ancient clock date from the thirteenth century. The dial is arranged on the Ptolemaic system of astronomy, which regarded the earth as being at the centre of the solar system. The earliest recorded repair was carried out in 1328. In 1760 a minute dial was added by Sir William Howard, 'an ingenious mechanic of this City'. The clock was fully restored in 1910.

Below: Cathedral Choir East in 1924. The magnificent east window beyond the choir was originally glazed in the fourteenth century. Damaged in the post-Reformation period, it was renovated in 1750 and 1770 with fifteenth-century glass from other parts of the Cathedral and further embellished with new glass. The medieval panels were removed for safety during the Second World War. The bishop's throne on the right, which was made in 1316, is 59ft high and is entirely constructed of wood without any nails.

Exeter Cathedral, Choir East.

Above and below: Two unusual views of Exeter Cathedral. *Above:* A 'hold-to-the-light' card of the Cathedral and Bishop's Palace from 1903. These cards were exported to Britain by W. Hagelberg of Berlin and show typical British views. When held to the light the perforations in the blue outer card reveal the creamy yellow card underneath to give a realistic impression of lit windows and a shining moon.

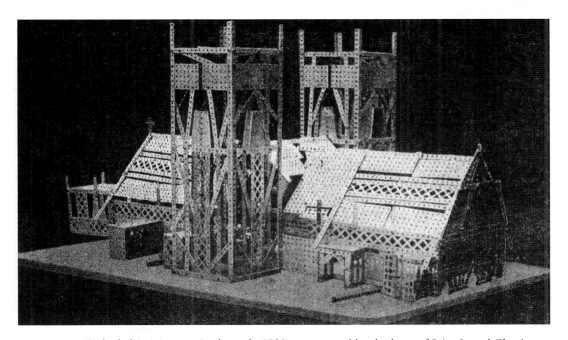

Exeter Cathedral in Meccano in the early 1930s, constructed by the boys of Saint James' Choristers Meccano Club under Mr M.C. Hodder. The model was complete with bells, electric light and a 'musical contrivance' resembling the organ. It was 5ft in length and had a height of 2ft 1in.

Above: The Hooker Statue unveiled on 25 October 1907. Made of white Purbeck marble and standing on a Dartmoor granite pedestal, the 7ft statue was the work of Alfred Drury. The statue was the gift of Richard Hooker, a descendant of Hooker's uncle the first Chamberlain of Exeter. His original donation was of a thousand guineas and anonymous. Unveiling the statue in the presence of the donor and other family members, the Bishop of Exeter said that Hooker was 'one of those great personalities round whom great movements and great institutions almost invariably embodied themselves.'

Left: The Hooker Statue, Cathedral Green, *c.* 1910. Born in Heavitree in 1553, Richard Hooker was educated at Exeter Grammar School, then ordained to Corpus Christi College, Oxford where he lectured for several years. He wrote many books, the most famous being the multi-volume work *The Laws of Ecclesiasticall Politie*, one of the greatest works of Anglican theology, which provided intellectual justification for Elizabeth I's Anglican Church. He died at Bishopsbourne, near Canterbury, where he was the rector, in 1600.

Right: Mol's Coffee House in 1930. One of the most visited sights in Exeter, it appeared on many postcards. Recent historical research has suggested that the 1596 pediment and the Elizabethan coat of arms derive from the ownership of John Dyer, who in 1595 had the lease of the building renewed by the cathedral authorities. Before 1660 the building served as the city's custom house, and it is likely that in 1596 it was reconstructed and a pediment erected with a coat of arms to indicate both the date of the building and its official function. By 1806 the pediment was removed, and the present one was installed in 1885. The Dutch gable was added at the top of the building in about 1879. Although it has long been claimed that Mol was an Italian, an authoritative recent study has suggested that the name could be derived from an abbreviation of Mary, the christian name of the first of seven women who ran the coffee house from the 1720s over a hundred year period.

OLD HOUSE.   EXETER.

Above: Mol's Coffee House in 1900. From 1898 to 1902 postcards were smaller and squarer in shape, with the front restricted to a vignette which left space on which to write a message. The address was written across the whole of the back of the card.

A painting of the panelled old oak room in Mol's Coffee House decorated with the coats of arms of famous Devon families, published by Worth in the 1920s. Worth's claim on the back of the card that this was the 'old club room of Raleigh, Drake and the other Armada admirals' was spurious, a fiction invented in the nineteenth century to promote the art gallery in the building. The rare star-shaped ceiling has slots integrated into the design that allowed huge picture frames to be lowered from the workshop above.

The Cathedral Yard in 1904. In 1657 the ancient burial ground of Saint Peter's Churchyard was levelled off and 100 trees from Duryard Wood were felled to provide wooden posts and rails to surround it. In the nineteenth century, the wooden rails were replaced by iron ones and these remained until 1939, when, all over Britain, they were removed to aid the war effort. The metal proved to be substandard and could not be used.

The Cathedral Yard in the early part of the twentieth century, taken from where the Globe Hotel stood until the Blitz of 1942. On the left is the impressive façade of the City Bank, established in 1786. The building, designed by John Gibson, was completed in 1877. In 1905 it was extended onto the frontage of the High Street. Beyond the bank is the building which, in 1932, became the popular restaurant and tea rooms, Tinley's.

The Cathedral Close in the mid-1950s. Central in the background is the Royal Clarence Hotel. Built as the Assembly Rooms in 1769, it was converted by a Frenchman, Pierre Berlon, into an hotel, the first in England to be known by this name. The Duchess of Clarence stayed there while visiting her husband in Plymouth, allowing it to take her name. When the duke became King William IV the hotel added 'Royal' to its name.

Above left: The view from the end of Saint Martin's Lane along the Cathedral Close towards Southernhay in the mid-1930s. The shop on the left is now the SPCK bookshop. At the foot of the shop front is a post commemorating the removal of Saint Martin's Gate in 1819, one of the seven gates that bordered the Cathedral Close. The dean and chapter agreed to the removal of the gate on condition that the lane 'be made a flat pavement for foot passengers only'.

Above right: The medieval Saint Martin's Lane in the mid-1940s. The Ship Inn, here advertising bed and breakfast, displays by its door the legend 'Next to my own Shippe, I love most that old Ship in Exon. A tavern in Fyssh Street' (an old name for Saint Martin's Lane), supposedly referring to a letter written to a friend by Sir Francis Drake in 1587. Recent revisionist research, however, has found that there is no evidence to support this claim. Other historical records show that the Parliamentarians in the English Civil War approved its cuisine: 'good wines, victuals and forage' was the verdict of troops billeted there.

Opposite: The Guildhall in 1912. One of the most popular subjects in Exeter for postcard publishers, a guildhall has stood on this site since about 1160. Reconstruction took place between 1468 and 1470, replacing a building of earlier date. The portico was built between 1524 and 1594 at a cost of £791 6s 7d. A massive new oak door was added to the hall at this date by the Exeter joiner, Nicholas Baggett, who was paid £4 10s for his labours. The main pillars of the portico are of Dartmoor granite and the rest of the façade is of Beer stone, now much repaired. In 1989, during cleaning and repairs, it was discovered that the façade was formerly brightly coloured with guilded capitals, with columns in black and red, banded with blue, red and yellow.

Exeter. Guildhall.

The interior of the hall in the Guildhall in 1912. The timbered roof dates from 1468 and the oak panelling of the hall was probably inserted in 1594 when the trade guilds contributed to the cost. There are eighty panels around the hall, showing coats of arms of past mayors and benefactors. The niche containing a bust of Queen Victoria was added in 1887 to celebrate her golden jubilee. The mayor's chair, underneath the large window (which was entirely reconstructed in 1772 by Exeter stonemason Edward Kendall), was made in 1697 but later heavily restored.

The Guildhall in July 1904 showing the suspended Lammas Fair Glove. The main function of the Guildhall over the past 800 years has been as a law court, but it was also the centre of the city's ceremonial life. On the third Wednesday in July the Sergeant-at-Mace paraded a long pole with a stuffed white glove decorated with flowers. Later this was suspended from the balustrade to proclaim the commencement of the Lammas Fair.

Advertising postcard for the Turk's Head public house in 1924. Above the name-plate is a carving of the head of a Turk from which the name derives. In 1289 the city authorities granted the owners the right to lean a beam against the adjacent Guildhall for the payment of one penny a year. In the late seventeenth century this was considered insufficient so it was doubled! A boot boy at the public house, frequently visited by Charles Dickens, was reputedly the prototype of his character 'the fat boy' in *The Pickwick Papers*.

Saint Peter's Corner, *c.* 1890. In an alcove stands the carved wooden statue of Saint Peter in a semi-crouching position, holding in his right hand a gothic church and in his left a Bible. He is treading on another figure, which represents paganism. Originally the figure helped to support the angle of a thirteenth-century house. By 1930 it was in a new position in the high street. Recently restored, it is now on display at the Royal Albert Memorial Museum.

Higher Market and Queen Street in 1910. Designed originally by George Dymond, it was continued by Charles Fowler (who had designed the Lower Market) after Dymond's death in 1835. It opened in July 1838 and closed in 1962, although the Doric columns have been incorporated into the new shopping centre. The covered, stone-built markets, each with its own water supply, were designed to improve standards of public hygiene after a devastating cholera epidemic in 1832.

Queen Street looking west in 1911. On the right are the premises of St Anne's Well brewery, wine and spirit merchants who occupied the site for eighty years from around 1890. On the left, on the corner turning into Paul Street is the Museum Hotel, which was demolished in 1926 to allow greater traffic flow in Paul Street. In 1932 it was replaced by the Information Bureau, a curiously shaped timber-framed building, which closed down fifty years later.

Right: The Clock Tower in 1905. Erected in 1897 to commemorate well-known philanthropist William Miles, it was unveiled on 21 April 1898 by his widow Louisa Anne Miles. Her late husband's concern for the welfare of horses was reflected by the inclusion of an elaborate drinking trough at the base. The comment on the front of the card refers to a simple obelisk, called the Quadrant, which previously stood on the site. The recipient was Miss Amy Scanes, who lived at the Old Bakery in Alphington, which was destroyed by fire in 1909 (see chapter five).

Below: One of the newly introduced trams passes the Miles Memorial Clock Tower in 1906. At the end of January 1951 it was the centre of a debate when a new road-improvement scheme would have meant its demolition. This was shelved after a protest campaign.

The Clock Tower, Exeter. Do you think this anything like the original one?

Exeter Clock Tower

Rougemont Castle, *c.* 1910. One of the earliest Norman fortifications, it was established in 1068 after William I captured Exeter at the end of an eighteen-day siege. After the Prayer Book Rebellion of 1549 it fell into decay, and was used nearly a century later as a strong point by the Royalists in the English Civil War. It was dismantled by the victorious Parliamentarians. Originally belonging to the Earls of Devon, it became the property of the Earls of Cornwall in 1232. In 1819 the castle and its adjoining site became the property of the county of Devon. The gate, the entrance to the inner bailey was constructed around 1770. The portcullis is for show only. The entrance to the left leads to Rougemont Grounds, at this time privately owned. Selected visitors were allowed in, but only on Thursdays and after scrutiny of their visiting cards by the owner.

Assize Court, Rougemont Castle in 1905. The Palladian-style court house was erected in 1774, in place of a 1607 sessions house. In the castle yard in 1655, John Penruddock, leader of an abortive Royalist rising against Cromwell's Protectorate was beheaded. In 1886 it was the scene of the first hot-air balloon ascent in Exeter, and later the first site of the Devon County Show. The central statue, by E.B. Stephens, is of Hugh Earl Fortescue, Lord Lieutenant of Devon, erected in 1863.

Rougemont Grounds in 1912. On 2 April 1912 the privately-owned grounds of Rougemont House were officially acquired by Exeter City Council. Formally opening the grounds for public use, the mayor, Dr C.J. Vlieland, expressed his pleasure and satisfaction on the acquisition of the beautiful grounds, which were once owned by the Duke of Cornwall. Now included in tours run by Exeter's Redcoat Guides, this picture appears to show a very early guided tour in progress.

The entrance to Northernhay Gardens, a popular venue for visitors, seen from Northernhay Place in 1907. The porter's lodge on the right was built in the late nineteenth century. The gardens are the oldest public gardens in England, having been converted into a walkway around 1612. Severely damaged in the English Civil War, when all the elm trees were felled, they were restored fifty-two years later. The statue of 'The Deer Stalker' shown on the following card can be seen in the distance.

The powerful bronze statue of 'The Deer Stalker' in Northernhay Gardens, on a card from 1915. One of the last statues completed by E.B. Stephens, it was first exhibited at the Royal Academy in 1876, when it was priced at £1,000. The sculptor, however, donated it to the city of Exeter and it was unveiled in 1878, to great public acclaim, in Bedford Circus. In 1880 it was moved to Northernhay Gardens.

A late autumn scene in Northernhay Gardens in 1905. The statue of Sir Thomas Dyke Acland, made of marble on a polished granite pedestal, stands by the lamp on the right. A long-time MP for Devon, Thomas Acland was a liberally inclined Tory, 'ever ready to protect the weak, to relieve the needy and succour the oppressed'. His family seat was Killerton House near Broadclyst. The statue was unveiled in October 1861 by the Earl of Devon. In the distance is the Volunteer Movement plinth, seen in the next card.

A band concert in Northernhay Gardens in 1909. Patriotic concerts were given in the gardens on Empire Day each year, sometimes at night when the grounds were illuminated. Seats were 3d each. The statue on the right is the Volunteer Movement plinth, of Dartmoor granite and Portland stone, which was unveiled in 1895 by the Duke of Cambridge. It commemorates Sir John Bucknill who, in 1852, formed a corps of citizen soldiers, the Exeter and South Devon Volunteers, the forerunner of the Territorial Army.

Matthew the Miller Clock, in the tower of Saint Mary Steps Church, a major attraction for visitors to the West Quarter, on a card of 1915. The central seated figure has a blue breastplate and a gilded plumed helmet. He holds a sceptre in both hands and bends forward on each stroke of the hour. The two figures on either side have plumed headgear and each carries a pike, a sword and a long hammer, which strikes the bell on which they stand. The figures are enclosed in a nineteenth–century alcove. Below them, the dial of the clock is decorated with reliefs, depicting the four seasons. A careful examination, conducted in the nineteenth century, concluded that the clock was locally made, but could discover no date of manufacture. However, several dates have been suggested by local historians, ranging from the sixteenth to the seventeenth century. The central figure was originally thought to be Henry VIII, but currently he is believed to represent a miller called Matthew who lived on Cricklepit Street, opposite Saint Mary Steps Church, whose punctuality helped his neighbours tell the time. In return, they erected the clock in his memory.

Right: Stepcote Hill in 1907. It took three horses to pull wagons up this medieval street, which was the main entrance to the city from the west until 1778, when a new stone bridge was built, which aligned with Fore Street. Many travellers on horseback ascended the centrally-guttered cobbled incline, including William of Orange in 1688, while pedestrians struggled up the steps. The surrounding houses had inadequate sanitation, and buckets were often used (although children frequently played among them in the street).

Below: West Street in 1904. Once prosperous, the area had become one of the poorest districts in Exeter by the early part of the century and in the 1930s the inhabitants were re-housed. This postcard provides an interesting social record of the period, as a gas lamp is serviced in front of a passing donkey cart, on the left, while to the right, a housewife buys fish as her washing hangs from the window-ledge above.

Left: A drawing of Bampfylde House, at the junction of Bampfylde Street and Catherine Street, published by Worths in 1910. Built in 1603, of local stone, it was used by the family as a private residence up to 1730. In the early 1930s it was acquired by Exeter City Council, and it opened as a museum on 7 November 1934. Internally rich in plaster ceilings, open stone fireplaces and oak panels, it was furnished by the city with articles of the Stuart and Jacobean periods, but it was sadly demolished after severe damage by bombing in 1942.

Below: Tucker's Hall in the early 1920s. Erected in 1471 as the chapel of the Assumption of the Virgin, of the Fraternity of Weavers, Tuckers and Shearmen, it became their business premises and was divided into two storeys in 1578. The upper floor, shown on the card, contains early seventeenth-century wood panelling and an original fifteenth-century barrel chapel roof. The building was considered unsafe in 1853 but escaped demolition. In 1905 its interior was restored and its exterior rebuilt in neo-Gothic style.

Tuckers' Hall, Exeter.

Right: Saint Mary Arches Church in 1930. A civic Church, it was the ancient parish Church of the Guildhall. The plain exterior, in a narrow back street, hides a fine Norman interior with round arches. There are numerous sixteenth- and seventeenth-century wall memorials, inscriptions and tablets dedicated to past mayors and dignitaries. Damaged by bombing in 1942, its elegant barrel roof was completely destroyed.

Below: The Tudor Room, Saint Nicholas Priory in 1905. Founded in 1087, the Church was demolished in 1536 at the Dissolution, and the domestic buildings sold. In 1913 the Priory was acquired by the city council, skillfully restored and opened to the public in 1916. One of the finest architectural features is the Norman undercroft. It is now a museum.

Exeter's underground passages in 1930 showing medieval lead pipe still in position. In the Middle Ages piped water was only available to the great institutions, especially religious houses, but in 1346 an agreement between the Cathedral, Saint Nicholas Priory and the city meant that Exonians received a third of the piped water supply. In 1420 this was augmented by a separate system, with pipes laid beside the existing Cathedral ones, from the springs of Saint Sidwell's across the Longbrook to the East Gate. Following a new course it led to a new fountain, the Great Conduit, a public showpiece in the centre of the road at the top of Fore Street. This was demolished in 1770. Between 1805 and 1833 the city passage at East Gate was deepened and the lead pipes replaced by cast iron ones. Following the cholera outbreak of 1832 the entire system was replaced but the supply to the Cathedral continued until 1901 and some of the original lead pipes remained. For many years a unique attraction for tourists, the entrance to the passages is now in Upper High Street.

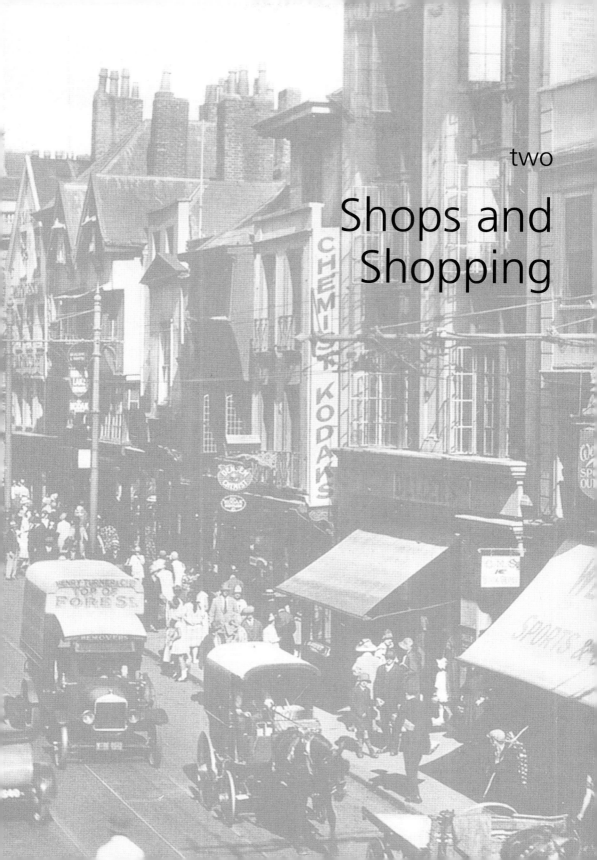

two

Shops and Shopping

Upper High Street from Castle Street, *c.* 1900. Although busy, the scene reflects the gentler pace of life possible in the years before the advent of trams and much later the car, when cycling was the newest popular form of transport and young children could gossip in safety standing in the road. The architecture is stimulatingly varied and the shops are almost exclusively privately owned.

High Street and Guildhall, *c.* 1906. The introduction of trams to High Street in April 1905 increased the pace of everyday life for Exeter's citizens, but they quickly adapted to the demands of their new environment. Although parts of the city had embraced horse trams since 1881, shopkeepers had opposed their use in the high street. However, on learning that passing horse cars had brought extra business to the Sidwell Street shops, they revised this decision and allowed motorised trams to be introduced.

Right: John C. Guest, 199 High Street, *c.* 1907. This modest shop front was the entrance to a large warehouse filled with an extensive range of pianos, whose makes included Bechstein and Collard & Collard. Customers were offered free carriage and tunings. Phonographs and gramophones could be taken in exchange. On Whit Monday 1907, competitors at the Exeter Cycling Club sports day were offered the opportunity to win the magnificent prize of a sixty-guinea British-made Brinsmead pianoforte, supplied by John Guest (who had been appointed their sole agent in January 1905).

Below: Domestic Bazaar Co., *c.* 1900. An early example of the one price shop: all items were priced at 6½d. Decorative lamps above the windows illuminated the goods on display at night, which were claimed to be the finest collection in Devon.

Timothy White Company Ltd, 63 High Street, in 1906. The Exeter branch of this national dispensing chemist opened on 5 December 1905, for the sale of pure drugs, chemists' articles and photographic goods of the very highest quality. Potential customers were promised that they could save from five to ten shillings in every pound on chemists' articles. Later the branch moved to 228 High Street. By the 1930s it also had an up-to-date library, offering for twopence new novels for three days and recently published ones for a week.

In 1927 another national retail chemist opened a branch in Exeter, when Boots moved to the corner of Queen Street and High Street. For many years the corner site was a favourite meeting place for Exonians. The building was taken over by sports specialists J. Webber in 1957, when Boots moved to a new building in Upper High Street. The opening of the new store was marred when the newly erected canopy collapsed and had to be rebuilt.

Right: J.A. Martin booksellers, 79 Fore Street, *c.* 1910. At one time this was the home of one of the first tourist guides of Exeter's underground passages, Mr Percy Martin. The building became the Chevalier Inn in the late 1930s, deriving its name from the famous equestrian statue on the roof. To the left is the cigarette factory of H.C. Lloyd, founded in 1784, which produced cigarettes, cigars, tobacco and snuff until the early 1920s. Both buildings were destroyed in the Second World War.

Below: A. Wheaton and Co. Ltd, 223 High Street in 1912. Alfred Wheaton, then head of Exeter's famous printing, publishing and bookselling business, acquired the lease of this store in 1886. Printing and publishing activities expanded rapidly, and in 1910 an educational showroom was opened. In 1927 the business relocated to 231-232 High Street, but when these premises were destroyed in the air raids on Exeter in May 1942, another shop opened at number 198. The firm's other premises, at 143 Fore Street, survived the war intact. The company remained a family business until 1966, when it merged with Robert Maxwell's Pergamon Press.

Tram No. 1 approaches Havill & Son, 5 High Street in 1905. One of Exeter's leading butchers, it was established that year and specialised in high quality English meat. Advertising assured would-be buyers that no-one could eat Havill's wholesome and appetising sausages without liking them. Next door, the Swiss Café restaurant (owned by E. Depaoli) offered chops and steaks, as well as tea, coffee and a variety of fancy boxes of chocolates and confectionery.

Exeter High Street in the 1920s, with cars now the dominant form of transport. The partially-timbered frontage centrally in view at 243-244 is ironmongers Wippell Bros and Row, established in the late eighteenth century and one of Exeter's oldest trading companies. The four-storied building had showrooms on the ground and first floors and specialised in heating, ventilation and electric lighting. Next door is the well-known grocers, the Devon and Somerset Stores, which claimed to be the largest and most complete store in the West.

The Cathedral Dairy Company, Eastgate in 1908. It was famous for clotted cream, which could be dispatched by parcel post twice daily. Fresh butter was churned daily and junkets made to order. A new department had just been opened providing milk-fed hams, bacon sausages and the Bologna sausage, polonies, made at their own dairy farm. Later the company was taken over by the Exeter Co-operative and Industrial Society.

Lipton's, 173 Fore Street in 1907. The eleven staff and the manager of this branch assemble outside a shop front packed with suspended sides of bacon and hams. At the lower level there is a fine display of butter and margarine and many varieties of tea. On the left-hand side of the postcard a notice offers free samples of tea and coffee to potential customers. The national grocery chain was founded in Glasgow in 1871 by Thomas Johnstone Lipton. Publicity, backed by sound stock at a fair price, made him a millionaire by 1880. Knighted in 1898, he became a baronet in 1902.

The General Post Office, High Street in 1909. Three-storied with a distinctive Gothic triple-arched entrance, it is seen on the centre left of this postcard in line with the approaching tram. Opened in 1885, it had been located in Queen Street since 1850. The building was enlarged in 1932. Normal working hours were from 7 a.m. to 10 p.m. on every weekday.

The interior of the High Street Post Office at the turn of the century. The building contained a spacious public area, sorting office and a first-floor telegraphic room, which was always open for business. A storeman and a caretaker were on the third floor. The building was completely destroyed in the air raids of 1942.

Right: J. & G. Ross of 227 High Street in the late 1940s. For many years this tailors and outfitters was one of the best-known in Exeter, catering for the needs of both men and women. They specialised in supplying complete outfits from suits, shirts and blouses to underwear. Dating originally from between 1660 and 1670, the building (which was built as a merchant's house) is still one of the finest examples of seventeenth-century architecture in the city. In the late 1950s and early '60s, both properties were threatened with demolition, but the façades remain, although the interiors were gutted.

Below: Pinder and Tuckwell, tailors, 20 Bridge Street. The four staff members pose against an impressive window display in 1900. The business was founded in 1824 by Mr R.R. Pinder, at 191 High Street; in 1872 he was joined by Mr J. Tuckwell, whose shop was at 32. Mens and boys outfitting was added to the original tailoring department. By 1933, it was established as one of Exeter's leading ladies and gentlemen's tailors and school-wear specialist. By now run by seven senior members of staff, it had also moved to 43-44 High Street. In 1969 the firm expanded into 45. In 1989, under new ownership, the firm moved to 83 Fore Street.

Pinder & Tuckwell, Clothiers, Bridge Street, Exeter.

Fore St Exeter, Looking East.   JWS 1623

WHOLESALE IRONMONGERS & MERCHANTS
109 FORE STREET, EXETER.
Our Mr. *Butter* will call *Friday* next.
YOUR ORDERS WILL VERY MUCH OBLIGE.

Above: A prominent '110' indicates the location of Walter Otton, the well-known Exeter ironmongers, in Fore Street in this card of 1909. Produced by a British postcard publisher, it was both printed and postally used in Belgium. A leading wholesale supplier of sheet and bar iron and steel, Ottons also catered for the early DIY market. A 1909 advertisement offered a washable distemper in 'all the newest artistic tints', which (with the addition of water) could treat a small room for one shilling. Ottons had a second shop on the other side of Fore Street at 135-6.

Left: Further up the hill, underneath the clock seen in the last card, Newcombe and Co. (at 109 Fore Street) was in direct competition with Ottons. This postcard, from about 1912, was used as the calling card of a commercial representative. The large building included twenty showrooms, displaying every description of ironmongery, together with ranges, grates, fireplaces, chimney pieces and scales, weights and measures.

Sidwell Street Shopping Week, October 1910. The Exonian Military Band is ready for action, while beneath them some of the organising committee pose for the camera. Decorated by day and illuminated by night, selected shops competed for the most attractive window. Trams carried advertising for the first time to promote the event. On the final Saturday, 22 October, local football team Exeter City held a benefit match against Plymouth Argyle in aid of the Shopping Week, winning by three goals to one.

Bakers C.J.S. Hill & Son of 19-21 Clifton Road lined up eight of their vans for the 1910 Shopping Week. The two newest were motorised. Hill's promised customers bread milled from the finest wheat the world produces, and the best and cheapest self-raising flour in the city.

Trams provided a new and excellent medium for advertising, as this card from the late 1920s demonstrates. The photograph was taken from the top deck of the following tram as No. 23 waited for No. 28 to come off the interlaced section in Fore Street. Colson and Co., Exeter's well-loved department store, was founded in 1792 by John Worthy Colson. Mrs Colson, a milliner, also sold silks and tea in the shop. Specialising in fashionable clothes, the store (one of the oldest in the West Country) was very popular with women of all ages, who bought new suits or frocks and then conversed with their friends in the tea lounge. Although the High Street premises were damaged during the war, the firm survived and flourished in the post-war period.

Mayor E.C. Perry drives Exeter's first electric tram on its inaugural
tour on 4 April 1905. The tram had just passed the Clock Tower on
its way to St David's station. The advertisement on the tram is a crude
fake and the lettering has been added to the negative. No advertising
was allowed on trams until 1927, although temporary permission was
granted in 1910 during Sidwell Street's Shopping Week. Green & Sons
costumiers and milliners, at 25-6 High Street, no doubt used this card
for promotional purposes.

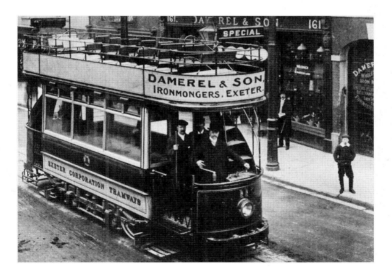

Another example of a card with the firms name added to the negative.
An originally blank-topped No. 11 tram photographed while passing
John Damerel & Son, wholesale and retail iron merchants, in about
1908. The fake lettering is, however, more neatly applied than on the
previous card. Damerel's shop in Sidwell Street held a wide range of
ironmongery, from steel joists to safety razors and scissors.

Above: In an age of keen competition no opportunity to advertise was missed. Two billboards on the wall of the fashion shop Maison de Modes, near the Eastgate Arcade, are seen in place of windows in this elegant card of the early twentieth century. Posters stuck to the balcony above show that some of the premises were to let. James G. Commin of 230 High Street was a bookseller of some note, who claimed to have the largest stock of books in the West of England. The firm also published, from its inception in 1900, *Devon Notes and Queries,* which in 1910 added Cornwall to its title, and was a valuable source of printed local history.

Left: An example of moveable placard advertising in Sidwell Street in 1909. The handcart is temporarily stationary, allowing the opportunity for a photograph. H. Samuels' branch at 211 High Street used outside advertising to back press advertisements which claimed that their display of watches, rings, necklaces and pendants could not be matched locally. The train fares of paying customers were paid up to a distance of thirty miles from the shop.

Cycling has long been a popular sport in this area and the Exeter Cycling Club was formed in 1873, making it one of the oldest clubs in Britain. The White Pearl Cycle Company's window at 16 New Bridge Street, seen here in 1906, had an impressive stock of cycles in the window, all fitted with Clincher tyres. Signs proclaimed a sale and bargains to be had as three enthusiasts, one perhaps the firm's owner, posed in the foreground.

As the twentieth century progressed, cycles gave way to the motor car as the most desired transport status symbol. Gould Bros Ltd certainly seem to justify their claim to have been pioneers of the motor industry in the west judging from this card of 1907, which shows their new showroom at the corner of London Inn Square and High Street. No cars are in sight and horses and carts negotiate the tram-lines. Latest models on display in the showroom included Darracq and Talbot, and second-hand models were also for sale. Gould Bros, officially appointed motor repairers to the RAC, also employed expert specialist mechanics for after-sales service.

High Street in the late 1920s. Cars compete with trams, motorised and horse-driven vans, carts and two cyclists for the limited road space as a policeman directs the traffic. The pavements are crowded as men and women, many wearing the latest cloche hats, spill out onto the road. The impressive premises of the city's best-known sports and games shop, Webber's, are on the right of the postcard. Their stock ranged from cricket, tennis and golf equipment, fishing tackle and guns to toys and games.

The Blitz of 1942 marked a watershed in the shopping atmosphere of the high street. Historic, individualistic and elegant buildings disappeared, as privately-owned shops were largely superseded by chain stores, and the rebuilt Upper High Street was greatly widened. In this postcard from the early '50s Marks & Spencer dominates the left-hand side of the street. The new store, opened in November 1951, replaced the original premises at 174-8 Fore Street, which had been bombed.

Founded in 1884 by Frederick John Cornish, the Exeter clothing firm moved to its landmark red brick Victorian building on the corner of Fore Street and North Street in October 1905. Later it became one of the largest and best-known mens and boys outfitters and tailors in the west of England. The ground floor is seen on the right of this postcard from 1909. The firm, run by descendants of its founder until 1981, survived the bombing of 1942 and prospered in the post-war period, but fell victim to recession in 1992.

George Walton and Co. opened a cash drapers, milliners and furnishing shop on High Street on Thursday 16 February 1905. By the early '50s, when this card was produced, the multi-department store had become a popular choice for shoppers, especially at Christmas, when the Fairyland Grotto was the highlight of the year for both children and parents. Chairs were provided at every counter in the store, which sold everything from china to clothes, and payment was made easy by a club card system.

Thomas Moore, gentleman's hosier, hatter and tailor, at 102 Fore Street in 1910. Moore opened his shop on 21 March 1907, providing great value for money and unsurpassed for variety, quality and style. Gas lighting, seen on the card, was installed in front of his shop. He later added a range of children's wear to the goods on offer. A promising and pioneering motorcyclist, he became a dispatch rider in the First World War and was killed in 1917. The shop survived the Exeter Blitz of 1942, expanding rapidly and adding a girls and ladies-wear range in the 1960s.

Exeter Co-Operative Society's store on the corner of Paris Street and High Street in the 1950s. The manager, Mr G. Bartlett, is seen on the right with a representative of Heinz as their products are unloaded from two vans. In the centre of the picture is Mr Don Lashbrook, a member of Exeter Postcard Society, then assistant manager. The building survived the Blitz, as incendiary bombs were successfully thrown off the roof by fire-watchers.

Right: An advertising card showing the new premises of F.W. Woolworth & Co's 3d and 6d department store at 190–191 High Street in 1934. Previously at 76–77 Fore Street, the company had taken over the site from Garton and King, who had occupied 190, and from Pinder and Tuckwell, who had traded from 191.

WOOLWORTH'S PREMISES, EXETER,
MONKS PARK STONEWORK
SUPPLIED AND FIXED BY
THE BATH & PORTLAND STONE FIRMS Ltd.

Below: WHSmith Ltd, at 233 High Street, was opened on Thursday 4 December 1952 by Colonel H.M. Llewellyn, who had won an equestrian Olympic gold medal that year at Melbourne, Australia, riding his horse Foxhunter. He was accompanied by another well-known rider, Pat Smythe. Would-be customers were invited to visit the new shop, which was 'laid out in the modern style', and were offered 'all classes of reading matter', as well as a library with books available on daily, weekly or subscription terms.

Left: East Gate Arcade in 1910. Many years before modern shopping centres were created, shoppers were able to avoid traffic and weather in one of the glass-topped arcades which were popular across Victorian Britain. Exeter's arcade, built in 1882, included a beautifully decorated oval window at its far end which faced visitors entering through an impressive arch from High Street. The elegant and popular shopping venue held twenty-two shops, ranging from the photographic studio that produced this card to optical lens specialists, chemists, hairdressers and a shop making umbrellas. Iron gates were lowered by a white-gloved officer to close the main entrance at the end of each day. The arcade was completely destroyed in an air raid in May 1942.

Below: Princesshay in 1961. Exeter's new pedestrian shopping mall, one of the first pedestrian precincts in the country, was laid out according to the recommendations of the post-war city planner Thomas Sharp. Officially named Princesshay by HRH Princess Elizabeth on 21 October 1949, it was designed to replace the East Gate Arcade and to provide a new shopping environment that had an uninterrupted view of Exeter Cathedral. The project took twelve years to complete.

PRINCESSHAY AND CATHEDRAL. EXETER.

HH 994

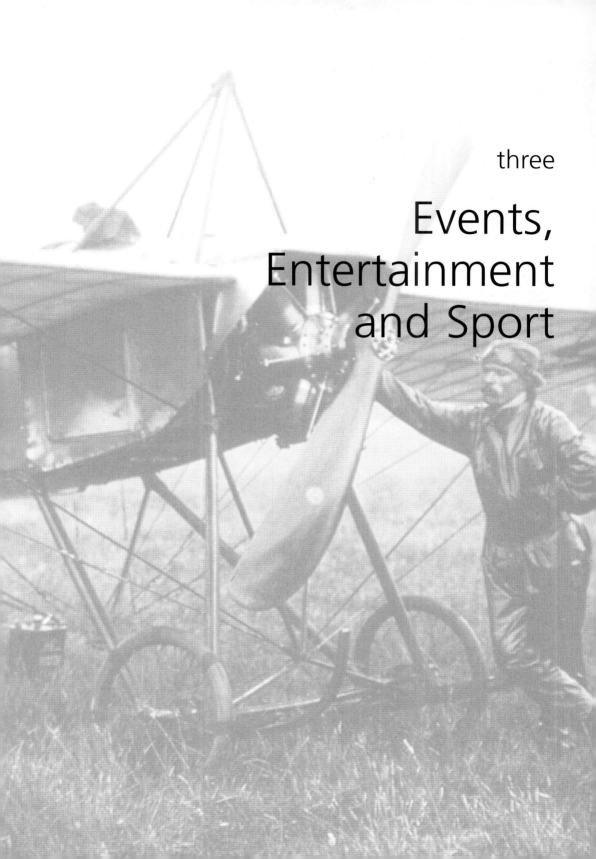

three

Events,
Entertainment
and Sport

MR CODY AT EXETER.

Samuel Franklin Cody lands his biplane, called a 'Cathedral' because of its wing structure, on 27 July 1911. Whipton in Exeter was a staging stop in the 'Daily Mail Round Britain Great Air Race', which was 1,010 miles long. Thirty competitors registered to fly the circuit from London to Edinburgh and back, via Glasgow and Bristol, navigating by a 22ft strip map of the route on rollers, which they unwound as the race progressed. Thousands of spectators waited three days to see the popular and flamboyant Cody arrive, the only 'all British outfit' and the only biplane left in the race. The previous night he had landed on the beach at Weston-super-Mare. Born Samuel Franklin Cowdery in Birdville, Texas in 1861, Cody changed his name to create a connection with the famous cowboy Samuel Cody, or Buffalo Bill. After a circus career he experimented with man-lifting kites, and by February 1905 he was employed by the British Army as an experimental aircraft and balloon designer, with the rank of Lieutenant and a salary of £1,000 a year. In 1909 he became a British citizen, largely in order to compete in flying events and competitions. He went on to win many competitions and died as he would have wished, swiftly in one of his own aeroplanes, crashing at Cove Common in Hampshire on 7 August 1913.

Frenchman Jules Vedrines with his seventy-horsepower Morane Borel monoplane at Exeter's Whipton airfield in the early hours of Wednesday morning, 26 July 1911. A crowd of about 15,000 people saw what was for most the entirely new sight of two planes at a height of about 1,500ft flying within a quarter of a mile of each other. Vedrines made a perfect landing at 6.47 a.m. He stayed for thirty-eight minutes, and was followed by his fellow countryman Jean Conneau, a naval Lieutenant calling himself Andre Beaumont, who eventually won the 'Round Britain Race' and the £10,000 prize. Vedrines was awarded a consolation prize of £200.

One year after the 'Great Air Race', Henri Salmet, the chief instructor at the Bleriot School at Hendon, lands at Exeter on 1 June 1912 in a fifty horsepower Bleriot X1. The visit was part of an aerial tour sponsored by the *Daily Mail*. Upon the outbreak of war in 1914, he returned to France and flew bombers with the French air force.

The proclamation of the accession of George V. A large crowd gathers at the junction of Belmont Road and Sidwell Street on 9 May 1910 to watch the imposing civic and military parade. The official proclamation was read by the Sheriff, Colonel G.M. Cardew. The procession, which included 250 soldiers and 100 cadets from Exeter School, started from the Guildhall and travelled to Saint Thomas, West Gate, Saint Anne's Chapel, East Gate and North Gate before reaching the front of the Cathedral.

Washington Singer Laboratories, University College of the South West, floodlit to celebrate the Silver Jubilee of George V, one of the many events in the city in May 1935. The building was built in 1931, mainly funded by a £25,000 donation from Washington Singer, a descendant of the founder of the Singer sewing machine company. Floodlighting in 1935 was provided by The Exeter Gaslight and Coke Company.

'General' William Booth, founder of the Salvation Army, on a visit to Exeter on 19 April 1911 to commemorate the thirtieth anniversary of the founding of the Exeter Temple. The crowded Victoria Hall gave the 'General' a standing ovation. Welcoming him to the city, the mayor contrasted the present enthusiasm with the hostility shown by Exonians to the Salvationists in the past century. The eighty-two year old 'General', speaking with great pathos and earnestness, addressed the audience for an hour and a half. This was to be his final visit to Exeter, as he died the following year.

Lord Bishop Archibald of Exeter lays the foundation of a new 500-seat brick-built church, one of the few in Exeter Diocese, at Polsloe Park on 6 August 1910. Designed by architects Harbottle & Son, it replaced an existing iron building. After giving a brief address to onlookers, the bishop was presented with a silver and ivory trowel and a mallet.

SALE OF WORK, PALACE GROUNDS JUNE 14, 1911   A

Sale of work at Bishop's Palace gardens, 14 June 1911. Held in aid of the Exeter Diocesan Association for the Care of Friendless Girls, the sale comprised twelve daintily decorated stalls laid out in a crescent shape in the picturesque palace grounds. Loaded with 'vari-coloured wares', they ranged from art and 'fancy work' of every description to a country-produce stall. The stalls were run by many local ladies, including the mayoress, who opened the sale.

Shakespearian Tercentenary. Exeter. May 1916.

Shakespearean tercentenary celebrations on 24 May 1916. Commemorations held at the Theatre Royal included a selection of scenes from *A Midsummer Nights Dream*. Bottom, seen here surrounded by some very attractive fairies, was played by amateur actor Colonel W.C. Richards. The local press acclaimed his performance as a 'striking success'. A second play, the appropriately martial and patriotic *Henry V*, starred Professor A.E. Dean as the King – one of the many University College staff and students whose knowledge, experience and enthusiasm was linked successfully with other performers.

Above: Some of the 400 participants in the historical pageant held in Bury Meadow on Wednesday 6 October 1909. Large crowds watched the re-enactment of the defeat of the Roman general Vespasian by the British King Arviragus at Exeter in AD 49. Wattle palisades represented the rudimentary defences of early Exeter. The surrounding bucolic scene was given extra authenticity by the addition of six sheep and two Devon cows. An evening performance was lit by 'powerful electric lamps'.

Right: Two floats of Saxon ladies, escorted by marching armed soldiers, in the procession through High Street, part of the historical pageant of 13 July 1910. The procession from Belmont pleasure ground to the County Ground, St Thomas was greeted along the route by many thousands of Exonians and visitors. The theme of the five performances at the County Ground represented the conflict between the Saxons and the Danes in Exeter, including the betrayal of the city by the Norman reeve Hugh. The pageant, organised by Mr C.J. Ross, featured 500 performers.

The marriage of Miss Nita Courtenay to Captain E.O.A. Newcombe of the Royal Engineers at Powderham Castle on 14 September 1909. Nita Courtenay, daughter of the late Hon. H.L. Courtenay, was given away by her cousin the Earl of Devon. The bride wore white ninon de soie, draped with silk French gillet embroidered in silver. After the reception at Powderham Castle, the bride and bridegroom, who was stationed in the Sudan, left for a honeymoon in Scotland.

The Bath and West Show under construction at Whipton in May 1909. Following the practice established forty years previously, Exeter hosted the Bath and West Society's show in the penultimate year of the decade. Funding the five day show, which ran from 26 May to Whit Monday (31 May) proved difficult because of agricultural economic recession. The tram service, however, which had been installed since the last show, helped to boost attendance figures. Admission cost seven shillings and sixpence. Timber and fittings from the show were offered at an auction on 1 July.

The Theatre Royal in 1908. Situated at the corner of Longbrook Street and New North Road, the theatre was rebuilt in 1889 after a devastating fire two years earlier, which had killed 186 people. As a direct result of the fire, new legislation was introduced requiring every theatre in Great Britain to install a safety curtain. The Theatre Royal was the first to do so. Additionally the new theatre was lit by electricity for the first time, and there were many safety exits. Although it flourished in the first half of the twentieth century, business declined after 1945 and the theatre closed in 1962.

The Hippodrome, London Inn Square in 1909. Formerly the Royal Public Rooms, the lease of the premises was acquired by the famous Exeter-born impresario Fred Karno, and Alfred Edwards. Karno redecorated it, reseated it and put in a modern stage, giving the builders only a fortnight to complete the work. Under Karno's management, which lasted for over ten years, the theatre staged many successful shows, starring many well-known artists, including Charlie Chaplin, Marie Lloyd and George Robey. The theatre later became the Plaza cinema. Bombed in 1942, it was engulfed by fire.

This elegant drawing shows the City Palace cinema, formerly a grocer's shop at the top of Fore Street, in 1912. Owned by a group of local businessmen, it claimed to be the 'home of bright and beautiful pictures'. By 1927 it (unusually) had a female manager, Mrs L. Williams, and in 1932 its name was changed to The Lounge. The building was destroyed in the Blitz of 1942.

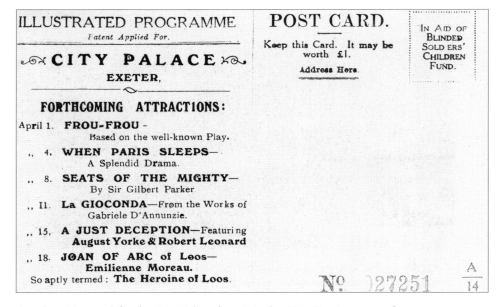

An advertising card for the City Palace from March 1916. Continuous performances were given from 2 p.m. to 10.30 p.m. and admission prices were 1s, 6d, and 3d. Tea was 'daintily served' from 3.45 p.m. to 4.15 p.m. Issued in aid of a fund for children of soldiers blinded in the First World War, this card was numbered for a prize-winning competition. The front featured a photograph of a Belgian airman, Adjutant E. Thieffry.

The Empire Electric Theatre, 248 High Street in 1912. Opened in August 1910, it was the first purpose-built cinema in Exeter and was owned by the Devon and Somerset Stores. Continuous performances were given from 2 p.m. to 10.30 p.m. with an entire change of programme every Monday and Thursday. Admission prices were 1s, 6d, and 3d with reductions for children before 6 p.m. Under the management of Mr J.H. Graham Cutts, it pledged to provide 'entertainment to suit the most fastidious' and to 'show the finest pictures the world produces'. It closed down in 1937 and the building was destroyed in 1942.

The Savoy cinema, London Inn Square in 1959. Opened on 22 November 1936, it was built on the site of the New London Inn Hotel. Although damaged it survived the bombing of May 1942, which destroyed the nearby Plaza cinema. Seating in excess of 1,500, it was a popular venue for cinemagoers. The film screened at the time of this photograph was the British comedy *Left Right and Centre*, with a cast including Ian Carmichael and Alastair Sim. By 1956 The Savoy was known as the ABC, but it carried both names after this date. In 1972 it became a bingo hall, which was demolished in 1987.

St Martins Church & Molls Coffee House, Exeter.

Above: Dellers, Cathedral Close in 1910. Originally occupied by the Exeter Bank, Dellers Café moved into the premises shown on the left-hand side of the card in 1906. It successfully expanded and opened new purpose-built premises in 1916 on the corner of Bedford Street and High Street. The building shown here is now part of the Royal Clarence Hotel.

Left: The impressive and ornately arched entrance to Dellers Café in Bedford Street in the 1920s. Built above an original single-storey structure occupied by Lloyds Bank, which spanned a corner site in High Street and Bedford Street, it was constructed by the Paignton-based company of Dellers. Hugely successful, the café (which opened in 1916) became the focal point of social life in pre-war Exeter. Although gutted by fire in 1942, it was so well built that demolition proved difficult.

The interior of Dellers in 1920. Its central feature was a two-tiered dining room which had its own palm court orchestra. Above it the elegant balconies were decorated with plasterwork adorned with classical cherubs. The capitals of the pillars had reliefs and the walls were wood-panelled. A number of curtained alcoves on the first balcony were available for private meetings, and an impressive staircase led into the dining room. Banqueting halls capable of handling large functions were available, and there was also a ballroom.

THE GLOBE HOTEL.   THE ONLY HISTORICAL HOTEL IN EXETER.   (FACING THE CATHEDRAL).

The Globe Hotel in 1910. The Globe was a seventeenth-century hotel in the Cathedral Yard, opposite the west front of the Cathedral and adjacent to St Petrock's Church. The front entrance porch was Georgian and its interior preserved the atmosphere of a coaching inn. It was gutted by fire in 1942 and demolished.

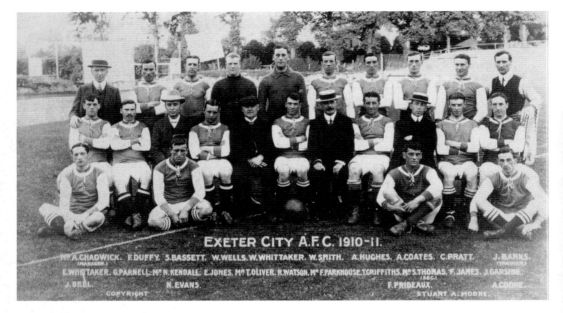

EXETER CITY A.F.C. 1910-11.

Mr A. CHADWICK. F. DUFFY. S. BASSETT. W. WELLS. W. WHITTAKER. W. SMITH. A. HUGHES. A. COATES. C. PRATT. J. BANKS.
(MANAGER.) (TRAINER.)
E. WHITTAKER. G. PARNELL. Mr N. KENDALL. E. JONES. Mr T. OLIVER. R. WATSON. Mr F. PARKHOUSE. T. GRIFFITHS. Mr S. THOMAS. F. JAMES. J. GARSIDE.
(SEC.)
J. BELL. N. EVANS. F. PRIDEAUX. A. COOKE.
COPYRIGHT STUART A. MOORE.

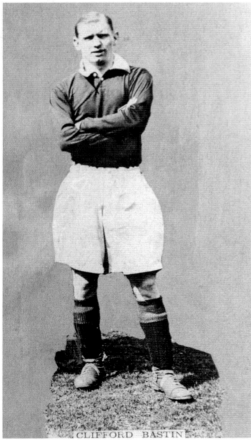

CLIFFORD BASTIN

Above: Exeter City AFC, 1910/11. A season of change for the football club formed in 1904. Beginning the season badly, they decided that their green colours were unlucky and changed to red and white. The 1910/11 season was the last to be played on the small original ground, which was extended in 1911 so as to be long enough for FA Cup ties, which had previously been played on the rugby ground. In 1910, Exeter had an official manager for the first time; Arthur Chadwick, seen here on the left in the back row. Top goalscorer was Jim 'Daisy' Bell (front row, extreme left). New goalkeeper Walter Whitaker (back row, centre) had played for Manchester United.

Left: Clifford Bastin, Exeter's most famous footballer, seen here in the early 1930s. Born in Exeter on 14 March 1912, he quickly became known as a goalscoring genius while still at school. He was picked for the English Schools side in 1926 (aged fourteen), and the following year he was playing for Exeter City reserves as inside left. By 1929, aged only seventeen, he was playing for Arsenal in the First Division. With them he scored 150 league goals and twenty-six in the FA Cup. He played twenty-one times for England. After retiring from football in 1947, he returned to Exeter as a pub landlord.

Devon versus Durham, April 1907. A crowd of 12,000 watched Devon play Durham in the Rugby County Championship final at the County Ground in Exeter. The game ended without either side scoring, and the teams shared the title.

Exeter Rugby Club First XV in 1913/14, the last season before the outbreak of the First World War. From left to right, back row: P.F. Spiller, W.G. Michelmore, F.H. Ball, R.F. Veale, C.L. Wills, W. Burns, B. Reed, L.J. Saunders, J. Hodge. Middle row: W.J. Butler, M. Tarbet, S.A. Chudley, J.C. Coombe (captain), J.B.C. Trafford, H.G. Parsons. Front row: E.C. Tudor-Jones, C. Hoare, C. Rew, B. Middlewick.

Exeter Cricket Club in 1931. Although probably founded much earlier, the club was re-inaugurated in 1858. No exact evidence of the number of fixtures arranged before 1950 is available, but it is probable that in the 1930s it was between sixty and seventy per year. Between 1930 and 1932 there was a small financial crisis as expenditure greatly exceeded income, but by 1932 fundraising and expenditure cuts had rectified the situation.

COUNTY CRICKET GROUND, EXETER.

The County Ground in 1910. From 1858 Exeter Cricket Club moved its ground three times. Although the last of these, at Gras Lawn, was regarded as one of the best in this part of England, and had been the club's home for eighteen years, it was inaccessible in comparison with the new County Ground. Additionally, the new ground offered a larger playing area of a higher standard with bigger pavilions and less annual expenditure, as the club now became a tenant instead of a landlord.

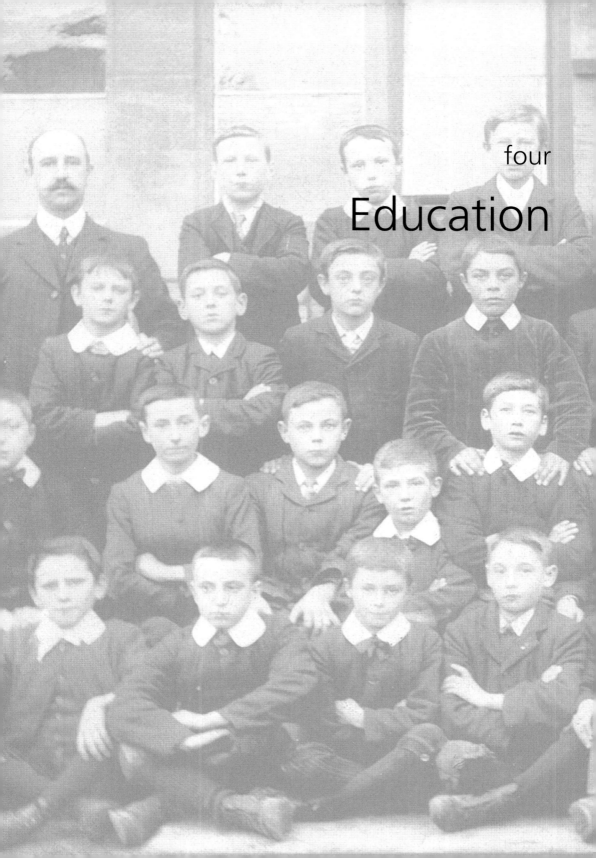

four

Education

Saint David's Boys School, Group 1 in 1903. The school had only two rooms, but 175 boys were taught in seven standards. The staff comprised two certified teachers, one of whom was the headmaster, Mr J.A. Pinn. They were supported by one uncertified teacher, two pupil teachers and one probationer pupil teacher. Their total annual salary was £403.

Saint Sidwell's Girls School, Class 1 in 1905. An HMI report in September of that year gave the school of 272 pupils a glowing write-up: 'This large school is in admirable order and is well organised and supervised. The teachers are hard working, capable and earnest so that the high state of efficiency recorded in previous years is being well maintained'.

Union Street School, St Thomas, May 1937. Coronation mugs and celebratory teas await children on the day of the coronation of George VI. The previous year, this had been denied to all as Edward VIII had abdicated before his coronation.

Union Street School, St Thomas, May 1937. The same hall is now full of children, but before they can sample the cakes there is the obligatory photograph. The solemn young lady with bowed collar and braided hair is Christine Trigger (née Darke), a member of Exeter Postcard Society.

Episcopal Modern School in 1932. Four charity schools, known as Episcopal Schools, were founded by the Bishop of Exeter, Offspring Blackall. Later there were only two, one for boys and the other for girls. The Episcopal Middle School for Girls, founded in 1876, moved to this newly-built school situated at Hill's Court, Pennsylvania in 1887. In 1920 its name was changed to the Episcopal Modern School, and in 1934 it was changed again to its much better-known name of Bishop Blackall School for Girls.

Episcopal Modern School science room in 1932. A new wing was built in May 1907 which contained science and domestic science classrooms, a valuable addition to the school. The extension was completed in 1912, adding an art room and three other classrooms. Both postcards were part of a set issued in the year Miss Jessie Headridge retired after more than thirty years as headmistress of the school.

Cathedral School Cadet Force in 1913. The building was first designed as a Diocesan training college and then used as a school for choristers, although a small number of other pupils were accepted. Situated at the south east end of Cathedral Close, it stood behind numbers eleven and twelve. The building was destroyed in 1942.

Hele's School in 1919. The site for the school was acquired from the city council in 1849, and the school was built at a cost of £1,000. It opened in January 1850. In 1919 the responsibility for the school was passed to a new body of governors, largely appointed by the city council. The number of pupils had risen dramatically over the previous six years, and by the time of this postcard had reached 445. The original grey stone building had only six classrooms. More classrooms and a gymnasium were added in 1909, and further extensions took place in 1932.

Exeter School in about 1919. Founded in 1633, the school moved to its Victoria Park Road site in 1880. The main school frontage, on the left-hand side of the postcard, was designed by the eminent Victorian architect William Butterfield, and built at a cost of £16,750. Classrooms are on the ground floor, dormitories above and servants' rooms in the attic. The chapel on the right, built in 1887, cost about £2,130. In 1919 the school numbered 194 pupils, sixty-one of whom were boarders. The railed-off area, which appears to be cultivated, later became the prefects' lawn.

EXETER SCHOOL SCHOOL HOUSE 1935

Thirty-five boarders at Exeter School pose on the quad for a group photograph in 1935. The headmaster Mr John Launcelot Andrews, sitting in the front row with his wife Elizabeth and their daughter Anne, lived on the premises from 1927 to 1937. He retired in 1949. Discipline in School House was strict. Unfortunate junior boys could be caned by the prefects, seen here in the front row, if sanctioned by the housemaster, who was at that time Mr J.H.T. Clarke.

Maynard School kindergarten at play in 1905. Pupils learned to read and draw in a pleasant room that had 'proper' desks and a canary. Outside they planted bulbs and played games on the small playing field. Minimum entry age was three, and the annual tuition fee for a child under eight was six guineas. Founded in 1876 as a girls school, by this time it included nine boys, some of whom are seen in this picture. In 1907 a School Inspector's report spoke of the valuable work done over the previous five years by the kindergarten in the early training of pupils.

Maynard School cricket First XI, 1932/33. One of a set of six school sports cards published for fundraising purposes. From left to right, back row: M. Phillips, M. Evans, H. Wonnacott, B. Wainwright, R. Self, B. Tojer. Second row: M. Simmonds, B. Matthews, R. Lamphorne, E. Matthews, M. Pattison.

Royal Albert Memorial Museum, Queen Street in 1905. In 1861, seeking a suitable memorial for Prince Albert (who had died that year), it was decided to construct a new building on ground donated by an Exeter MP, in Queen Street. The new structure, designed by John Hayward, incorporated the existing School of Art and added lending and reference libraries, a reading room and a museum. The foundation stone of the new institution was laid in 1865, and it was completed in 1870.

The Zoological Room of the Royal Albert Museum, *c.* 1915. Many collections of zoological interest have been acquired by the museum, including the Peel and Bradshaw Collection of great game animals, hunting trophies from Sir Samuel Baker, a tiger shot by George V in 1913, the Linter Collection of land shells and the Champerdowne Collection of British fossils.

University College, Gandy Street, in 1915. Built at the rear of the Royal Albert Memorial Museum in 1911, it cost £24,500. Originally part of the museum, the college became a university college in 1901 and rapidly expanded. Following the development of the Streatham estate, first presented to the college in 1922, this building became a centre for the arts and those reading sciences moved into new buildings. The iron railings were removed as part of the war effort during the Second World War. It is now the Phoenix Art Centre.

Female students outside University College in the 1920s. The first college hostel for women was opened as early as 1906. Examination results from 1908 and 1909 show women studying a wide variety of subjects, gaining science qualifications at degree and inter-BSc level, although the more 'practical' subjects at City and Guilds level were still male dominated. The number of female students at the college rapidly expanded in the 1920s, a fact demonstrated by the opening of two more hostels for women – Hope Hall in 1924 and Lopes Hall in 1929.

Students from Exeter College in 1910 pose for a Rag Week photograph dressed in a wonderful array of hats and outfits. Even one motorbike has a mask with a cigarette hanging out of its mouth! The students on the right are obviously expecting a large response from the public, judging from the number of collecting tins they are clutching.

The more formal approach to fundraising was adopted by the University of the South West in the 1920s. This card was one of a series of twenty-four which helped raise money for the 'Building and Endowment' fund. In 1922 Alderman W.H. Reed, a successful businessman committed to the life and work of the city, had presented the college with a substantial part of the Streatham estate together with the Italianate villa of Reed Hall.

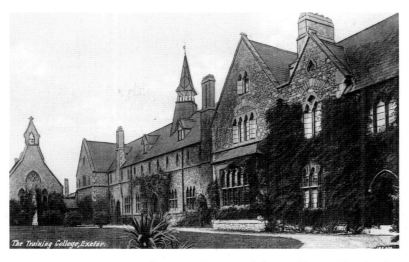

Exeter Diocesan training college in 1908. Founded in 1839 as a Church of England training college for schoolmasters, the college was originally based in Cathedral Close. On Saint Luke's Day (18 October) in 1854, the premises shown on the card were officially opened by Bishop Phillpotts as the new college building. Students, who were all male, each had an individual room, although it was unheated and sparsely furnished. The regime was strict; the authority of the principal was undisputed and much emphasis was placed on prayers and worship, which were obligatory before breakfast and on Sundays. In 1930 it was renamed Saint Luke's College. Badly damaged by bombing in 1942, it was partly repaired after the war. In 1978 it became the School of Education of Exeter University.

The dining hall at Saint Luke's College in 1937. This elegant dining hall replaced one which, in keeping with the original authoritarian regime, had long trestle tables. In 1939 it became a British Restaurant for the supply of cheap basic meals to the public. It is now a drama school and part of the School of Education theatre.

Deaf and Dumb Institution in 1910. Founded by Mrs Hippisley Tuckfield in 1826, the original premises were in Alphington. Next year the purpose-built structure shown here was erected 'upon a delightful elevation in Topsham Road'. In 1897 the property was extended at a cost of £6,023, and could then accommodate eighty-six boarders. Further extensions were carried out from 1947 onwards, and by 1969 all previous structures had been demolished and rebuilt. It is now the Royal School for the Deaf.

Some of the staff and pupils at the Deaf and Dumb Institution in May 1907. Accounts published in the following year show that there were fourteen scholars at the school, twelve teachers or officers and thirteen servants. Board for them amounted to £1,028 16s 11d. The majority of the cost of the maintenance of the school was covered by an annual grant from the Board of Education and from local rates.

five

City in Crisis

The wreck of tram car No. 12 on Exe Bridge, 7 March 1917. Travelling from Heavitree to Dunsford Hill at 11 a.m., the tram went out of control down the steep incline of Fore Street. The driver, Charley Saunders, had the brakes full-on but they became de-wired and the tram continued to accelerate, colliding with a horse-drawn delivery wagon carrying tobacco and matches which was pulling out to avoid a kerbside barrow. The driver escaped death but the horse was killed. The tram conductress, Mrs Harle, jumped off in Bridge Street and escaped injury. Eyewitnesses saw women passengers 'moving about the car in distracted fashion' as it careered downhill. Miraculously another crash was avoided as a tram coming up Fore Street rushed on to the double tramlines. Charley Saunders, an ex-coachman, managed to keep his violently-swaying tram upright until it reached Exe Bridge where it left the rails and, swerving to the right, hit the bridge parapet and turned over. The forty-two seat tram had only five passengers on board – four women and a fifteen-year-old boy, Alfred Snow. Four were injured, but sadly one lady, a Mrs Findlay, was killed. The damaged tram was lifted, towed back to the depot and eventually scrapped in 1921.

Tram accident at Exeter 7-3-17

Police, tram officials and a crowd of onlookers at Exeter's most publicised tram crash on 7 March 1917. At the corner of the bridge, under the lamp-post, the capped man clutching a parcel is William Escott, grandfather of Exeter Postcard Society member Christine Trigger. William's wife, Mary, was at home waiting to make brawn for dinner from the sheep's head which was inside the parcel he clutched. She did not believe the reason for his late arrival until she saw this postcard of the accident.

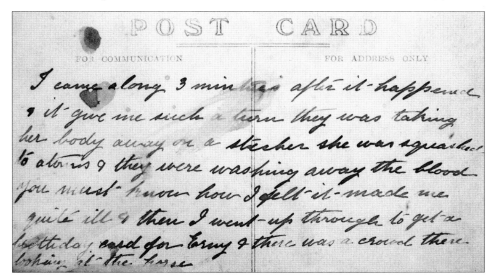

'I came along three minutes after it happened and it gave me such a turn, they was taking her body away on a stecher she was squashed to atoms and they were washing away the blood'. An important eyewitness account of events after the crash. Mrs Findlay had been thrown off the tram and killed instantly as she fell onto the road. Her husband, a local decorator, only learned of her death four hours later.

Traction engine accident on Fore Street, 25 April 1906. As a traction engine pulling two trucks filled with bricks travelled down Fore Street, the vehicles skidded and started to run downhill. Prompt action by the traction engine driver averted a serious accident. Turning his machine at a near right-angle to the road, he blocked one truck from running downhill. The second truck had already tipped over, spilling its load onto the road. The local press suggested that the accident was caused by the granite setts laid for the lines of the tram system, which had opened the previous year. At a meeting of Exeter City Council on the same evening, it was decided to introduce new regulations prohibiting traction engines from travelling down Fore Street. Although the council's action appeared to be prompt, the steepness of Fore Street had long given cause for concern. On 18 October 1905, thirty-six tradesmen in Fore Street and Bridge Street had petitioned the council to take 'immediate steps to prevent traction engines from ascending or descending Fore Street hill.' They pointed out that serious accidents would take place and that there had been 'no less than three runaway traction engines in the last three months.' The matter was referred to the Streets Committee on 25 October and a surveyor was asked to report on the best means of 'obviating the slippery conditions of this hill'. New draft by-laws were drawn up in November but not brought into effect.

Fire at Alphington on 13 February 1909. The outbreak occurred between three and four o'clock in the afternoon but it was some time before the fire brigade was called. All the properties were thatched and fire spread rapidly. Handicapped by lack of water, which had to be drawn from the Alphin Brook about a quarter of a mile off, the firemen failed to save the houses affected, but there was no loss of life. The local press reported that 'flames leapt aloft in a most menacing manner and as night fell a spectacle of lurid magnificence was presented'.

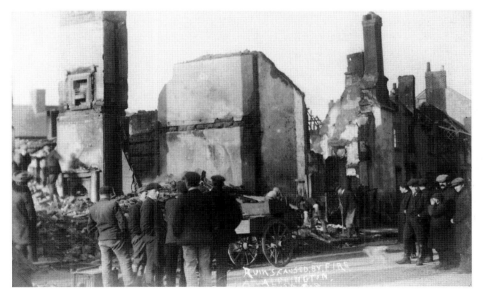

The aftermath of the fire at Alphington. Nine houses were destroyed in the fire, the worst in the area for thirty years, including the old bakery, one of the oldest local businesses. Although most of the furniture was saved, about forty people were rendered homeless and damage was estimated at the then considerable sum of over £2,000. A subscription list was opened for the house occupiers, administered by a committee of the parish council.

In the early afternoon of 1 June 1910 a disastrous fire devastated two timber yards and two stores and offices, over an area of one acre below Queen Street, adjoining the railway. Train and tram services were suspended as burning pieces of wood set roofs alight. The wind direction blew the flames away from the prestigious Victoria Hall, seen in the centre of the picture, but towards the City Hotel. Nineteen jets of water, poured onto the flames by the fire brigade, saved the hotel but the damage estimate was £10,000.

The aftermath of the Victoria Hall fire on Queen Street, 6 October 1919. The fifty-year-old hall (the largest in Exeter) was burned down in the early hours of the morning in spite of the combined efforts of six fire brigades from the city centre and branches, supported by one from the railway. Damage estimated at £6,000 included a £2,000 organ, which appeared to be 'playing' as heat forced air through its pipes. The local press suggested that smokers at a meeting held the previous night to discuss the end of a railway dispute had inadvertently caused the fire.

Superintendent William Pett and a steam-operated fire engine pump from the Exeter fire brigade in 1910. Born in Sevenoaks, Kent, William Pett joined the fire service there at age fifteen. His family had a long history of fire fighting. As far back as 1604, one of his ancestors, Phineas Pett, shipwright to James I, designed a system for the extinction of fires at sea. His grandfather was one of the first members of the Sevenoaks Fire Engine Association, established in 1826, and his father was a member for over thirty-six years. As Chief Fire Officer of Exeter's fire brigade for forty years, William Pett was the public face of the reliability of the service. He led his men from the front, as exemplified in the press reports, like that of a serious fire in Exeter in 1910 when 'crawling on hands and knees he located the scene of the fire' and, in an earlier fire in 1909, 'Superintendent Pett had a narrow escape while working in dense smoke in a lift hole'. He truly deserved the mayor's praise when awarding him, in 1911, the Fire Association Medal for long service; 'One thing that made them feel safe in their beds it was to know that they had so efficient a Chief Officer of the Fire Brigade'. He retired in June 1927.

Devon Reserves Parade. Aug 7th 1914

Don't worry, I'll soon be back.

Above: After German troops crossed the Belgian border, ignoring Britain's request to respect the neutrality of Belgium, war was declared on 4 August 1914, honouring a treaty of 1839. Three days later, Devon Regiment Reserves marched through the High Street, crowded with enthusiastic Exonians, to join the reservists mobilised across the nation. The mayor received a request from the Higher Barracks to dissuade over-eager citizens from offering the soldiers intoxicating drinks. The reservists left by train the following evening between seven and eight o'clock, from Queen Street station.

Left: 'Don't worry, I'll soon be back'. Postcards like this one comforted those who were left behind in 1914 when soldiers went off to fight. Almost everyone, from the King downwards, was convinced that the war would be over by Christmas. Lord Kitchener, however, planned for a three-year conflict.

Part of Kitchener's new Army at Exeter.

Above: A long line of Exonians march four abreast to join Kitchener's 'New Army' in 1914. Soon after the outbreak of war it was apparent that Britain's army of regular soldiers, territorials and reservists needed to be rapidly augmented. Lord Kitchener embarked on a propaganda campaign which raised a further 100,000 men in the first month; his famous finger-pointing posters were supported by postcards and local press advertising. Service for recruits aged between eighteen and thirty (later thirty-five) was expected to last three years. Many much younger recruits joined up in order not to miss the 'war to end all wars'. By mid September 500,000 had enlisted, including 2,369 in Devon.

Right: If an appeal to patriotism failed, psychological pressure was used to shame men to enlist, as cards like the one on the right from early 1915 demonstrate. Harold Begbie obviously expected everyone to return quickly and safely, but mounting casualty figures proved him wrong as the war dragged on. By 1916 conscription was introduced, as disillusionment was starting to replace patriotic fervour.

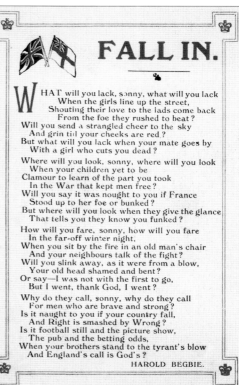

FALL IN.

WHAT will you lack, sonny, what will you lack
  When the girls line up the street,
  Shouting their love to the lads come back
  From the foe they rushed to beat ?
Will you send a strangled cheer to the sky
  And grin till your cheeks are red ?
But what will you lack when your mate goes by
  With a girl who cuts you dead ?

Where will you look, sonny, where will you look
  When your children yet to be
Clamour to learn of the part you took
  In the War that kept men free ?
Will you say it was nought to you if France
  Stood up to her foe or bunked ?
But where will you look when they give the glance
  That tells you they know you funked ?

How will you fare, sonny, how will you fare
  In the far-off winter night,
When you sit by the fire in an old man's chair
  And your neighbours talk of the fight ?
Will you slink away, as it were from a blow,
  Your old head shamed and bent ?
Or say—I was not with the first to go,
  But I went, thank God, I went ?

Why do they call, sonny, why do they call
  For men who are brave and strong ?
Is it naught to you if your country fall,
  And Right is smashed by Wrong ?
Is it football still and the picture show,
  The pub and the betting odds,
When your brothers stand to the tyrant's blow
  And England's call is God's ?

HAROLD BEGBIE.

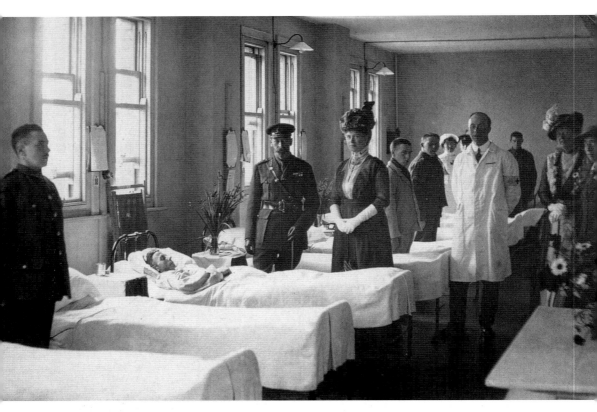

George V and Queen Mary visit temporary military hospital no. 1 – the West of England Eye Infirmary – on 8 September 1915. It was the first visit of a reigning monarch to Exeter in time of war since Charles 1, in 1643, in the middle of the English Civil War. Although strict press secrecy was maintained, news of the visit leaked out and the route from Saint David's station to the hospital was crowded with Exonians of all ages. Five cars conveyed the Royal visitors and other dignitaries to the hospital where they were received by Miss Georgiana Buller, the only daughter of the late general, who was the Deputy County Director of Devon's Voluntary Aid Organisation. The royal visitors saw every ward and chatted to patients for three quarters of an hour. Before leaving, the King gave a speech declaring his pride in the way every soldier had fought and expressing his hope for their swift restoration to health. The King and Queen then visited hospital no. 5 in Castle Street to meet other wounded soldiers. One of these, Private G. Bidgood, was presented with the DCM in recognition of his heroic action in the Dardanelles. The royal couple departed on the special royal train at 1 p.m., en route for Plymouth. After the visit, all wounded soldiers who could be moved, together with others from other parts of the county, about 900 people in all, were given lunch at the Victoria Hall.

Anzac Day parade outside the west front of the Cathedral, 25 April 1917. A special service was held in the morning for about eighty wounded Australian soldiers, commanded by Captain H.B. Beavis and Lieutenant J.C. Browning. After the service a crowd assembled to witness their departure from the Cathedral and their arrival at the Guildhall, where a reception was given by the mayor, Mr James Owen. Flying over the Guildhall was the Union Jack presented to the city by the children of Exeter, South Australia.

Gallantry awards being presented at a ceremony held in Northernhay Gardens on the afternoon of 7 May 1918, by Lieutenant-General Sir H.C. Sclater, Commander in Chief, Southern Command. Among the large gathering at the event were representatives of a number of regiments and cadets, together with the Lord Lieutenant of Devon, the Lord Bishop of Exeter, the Bishop of Crediton and the mayoress. Medals awarded to fallen soldiers were collected by widows, parents and young sons.

German Guns at Exeter.
Captured by the 8th & 9th Devonshire Regt. at Loos.

EXETER WAR MEMORIAL.
CREEPING EXETER

Above: Two captured 77mm German field guns on display in Northernhay Gardens, 13 November 1915. On 26 September the 8th and 9th Battalions of the Devonshire Regiment overcame heavy German resistance to capture eight guns during the Battle of Loos, north of Hulluch. Two of the guns were shipped to England and, at a ceremony held outside Queen Street station on 12 November, they were handed over to the Lord Lieutenant of Devon, Earl Fortescue, by Colonel Walsh of the War Office. Paraded through the city, they returned up Fore Street on their way to Northernhay Gardens. The mayor, who received the guns on behalf of the citizens of Exeter, took the salute of the troops as the procession of soldiers and mounted constables passed the Guildhall.

Left: Exeter War Memorial in Northernhay Gardens, 11 November 1923. The 31ft memorial had been unveiled earlier that year by the Right Honourable Admiral David Beatty, on 24 July. At its base four magnificent bronzes of a nurse, a prisoner of war, a soldier and a sailor surround a central plinth, on the summit of which Victory stands triumphant with her foot on a slain dragon. The bronzes were sculpted by John Angel, who spent most of his early life in Exeter.

Above: In the early hours of the morning of 4 May 1942, in the second of the major German air raids on Exeter, supposedly in revenge for the RAF attack on Lubeck, about thirty Junkers 88 bombers dropped 160 high-explosive bombs and 10,000 incendiaries. Wind blown, a massive inferno rapidly destroyed many areas of the city, including the upper part of the High Street. 161 Exonians died and 476 were injured. The scene here from the interior of the destroyed Cathedral Dairy shows the devastated façade of the Plaza cinema, later demolished, together with the Savoy, which survived despite being damaged.

Right: Exeter Cathedral was damaged by a 1,000lb high-explosive bomb on 4 May 1942. The chapel of Saint James, its crypt and muniment room were destroyed, together with the South Quire Aisle. Although the organ was wrecked and most of the glass shattered, other treasures had been taken to safety. Two of the flying buttresses were destroyed but the others, with steel underpinning, saved the Cathedral from collapse.

Clearing the central area of Exeter on 4 May 1942. Some of the 5,000 men drafted in to help, many of them soldiers, at work on the wreckage of Bobby's next to Saint Stephen's Church. A wartime diarist from Exmouth described her shock on visiting Exeter after the Blitz: 'I walked round what used to be peaceful and beautiful Exeter, it was an awful sight. I could not believe my eyes at first. From Lyons right up into Sidwell Street it was flat as far as I could see. No shops, no Church, nothing at all. Bobby's shop and Lloyd's Bank were empty shells'.

The gutted Barclays Bank building stands starkly in Bedford Street, one of the most severely damaged of Exeter's streets. Alongside it Martin's Bank was destroyed and on the opposite side of the street another bank, Lloyd's, was badly damaged as the economic centre of the city was severely hit. However, above Lloyd's was the loss most keenly felt by Exonians – the city's social centre, Dellers Café.

Children watch the River Exe in flood in January 1918. In the background on the left is the transit shed, built in 1820, which was used to provide undercover storage for cargo being transferred to and from sea-going vessels alongside the quay. By it, on the right, tower the massive warehouses built in 1835 of red Heavitree sandstone, which were used to store goods. The location was used in the 1970s BBC television series *The Onedin Line*, representing the port of Liverpool in the early 1860s.

The River Exe in flood at Weirfield Road in January 1918. Although this flooding was the worst recorded since 1894, flash floods were frequent. In October 1910, after heavy rain, the sewers were unable to carry away the volume of water, and Cowick Street, Alphington Street and Okehampton Street were flooded. The council surveyor concluded in his report that the cost of installing drainage to prevent flooding like this would be prohibitive and that 'he had no remedy to advise for preventing the occurrence in the future'.

A policeman rows two women and a child to safety along flooded Cowick Street on 27 October 1960. After nearly a month of heavy rain, followed by over 2.4in on the previous day, the River Exe burst its banks and a miniature tidal wave engulfed Alphington Street, Cowick Street, Okehampton Street and Haven Road. Exe Bridge was closed and traffic diverted as hundreds of houses and shops were flooded. Local people, stranded by the frightening speed of the floodwater, were rescued from their homes by boat and lorry in Exeter's worst flood of the century.

This view from Exe Bridge shows water surging from the River Exe into Okehampton Street on 27 October 1960. On 3 December, after a heavy downpour of three inches of rain, flooding reached up to 6ft deep. Following the disastrous floods in 1960, Exonians demanded action to avoid future flooding. After careful consideration of options, the River Exe Flood Alleviation Scheme was started in 1965 and completed in 1979, and has so far proved successful in preventing flooding in low lying areas of the city.

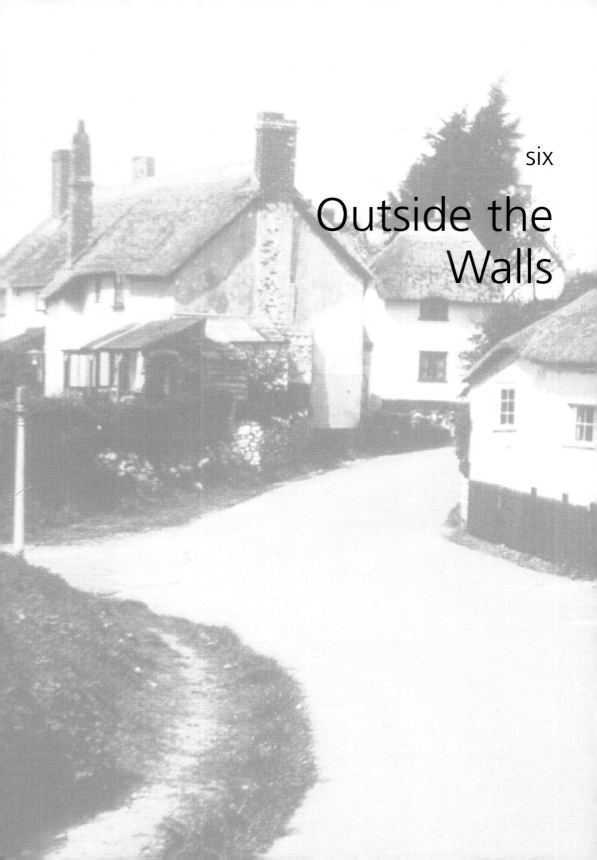

six

Outside the Walls

Cattle auction at the livestock market in Bonhay Road in about 1904. The auctioneer stands under the canopy with his assistants, as the bowler-hatted farmers and butchers examine the long-horned cattle on offer. Cattle and pig markets were originally held in the high street, where they were regarded as 'a notorious grievance,' before being removed to Bartholomew Street in 1691. They remained here for over 125 years, still 'a sad nuisance to the great discomfort of the neighbouring houses', before they were eventually sited in Bonhay Road. In 1932, Exeter City Council discussed the possibility of enlarging the Bonhay Road site to include a public abbatoir, then in Tudor Street, but this was rejected in favour of a market at the corner of Marsh Barton Road and Alphington Road which, when opened in 1939, brought about the closure of the Bonhay Road site. Later, in 1991, this last site closed and the present site near Matford was opened.

42 EXETER. — Ex Bridge. — LL

A bowler-hatted shepherd drives sheep over Exe Bridge to the Friday livestock market in
Bonhay Road in 1905. With the increasing traffic on the new bridge after the introduction
of trams and more use of railway traffic, sheep and cattle were more likely to travel from Saint
David's Station straight down Bonhay Road to the market. However, driving livestock from
the countryside outside Exeter through the streets was still known to occur, even as late as
1939, when the market had moved to Alphington Road.

Exe Bridge seen from Saint Thomas in 1906. A crowded bridge leaves little room for the
movement of livestock as horse-driven carts and carriages compete for road space with the
No. 3 tram from the newly-introduced service. The City Brewery is partially seen on the
right of the picture in the background.

Rowing on the canal in 1907. At the top left is the entrance to the wet dock or basin, constructed to take large-capacity vessels. It was opened on 29 September 1830, with great festivities, watched by local dignitaries and hundreds of spectators. In 1969 it became the venue for the Exeter Maritime Museum, which held a comprehensive collection of boats and was a major tourist attraction. It closed in 1997. On the right of the card is the outlet to the River Exe.

Dorothy's boating stage entrance in Bonhay Road in 1920. Rowing was one of the most popular activities for Exonians in the 1920s. Situated on the banks of the River Exe near the cattle market in Bonhay Road, the leisure boat business, owned by the Dorothy brothers, offered a wide choice of boats for hire for a half hour or an hour. The landing stage was rented from the city council.

The Quay and Rope Ferry.   Exeter

Quay and rope ferry in 1905. A ferry has operated from this point since 1641. The ferryman uses his hands along a waist-high rope, latterly a wire, to propel the boat and its passengers across the river. It is now called Butt's Ferry after George Butt, who campaigned successfully to save the service in the 1970s, when the city council approached the Government to obtain an Act of Parliament to have the ferry closed.

The Custom House in 1914. The oldest surviving brick public building in Exeter, built in 1681 and occupied by customs officers until September 1989. The port of Exeter had responsibility for all ports from Teignmouth to Lyme Regis. Celia Fiennes, visiting Exeter in the late seventeenth century, described the upstairs 'Long Room', which has an outstanding baroque plaster ceiling, as being 'full of desks and little partitions for the writers and accountants, full of books and files of paper'. The building was externally restored in 1992.

The roofed interior of Saint Thomas station in 1920 as a train arrives before heading off for Saint David's station. Soon after the first train steamed into Saint David's from Paddington on 1 May 1844, a second station was erected in the large suburb of Saint Thomas. Railway excursions began almost immediately and, by 1846, Exonians could travel by train to Dawlish, which rapidly became a favourite seaside resort for many. Cheap train fares on Sundays enabled the poorer inhabitants of the city to travel to the sea on their day off for the first time. By 1859 as many as 350 travelled on the 'sixpenny dip' concessionary train to the Dawlish beaches, but better-off visitors were outraged by the perceived unconventional behaviour of the new day-trippers, who often could not afford costumes or a bathing machine! Cheap-day Sunday excursions continued however, well into the next century. In 1903 the Exeter, Teign Valley and Chagford Railway, a new branch line, was inaugurated when its first train left Saint Thomas station at 3.40 p.m. on 1 July. Known later as the Teign Valley line, it stretched to Heathfield and operated until 9 June 1958, when it closed as a passenger service.

Old parish stocks in Saint Thomas' Churchyard in 1910. Public humiliation in the parish stocks was used as a punishment in early modern England, especially by the Church Courts. Moral offences meriting this treatment included sex before marriage, giving birth to illegitimate children, incest and adultery. Feet locked in position, victims were subjected to verbal and physical abuse from their neighbours until they were judged to have atoned for their sin.

Saint Thomas Pleasure Grounds in 1913. Opened on 10 March 1891, the four-acre park was laid out with walks and flower-beds at a cost of £3,600, paid for by the Saint Thomas Local Board of Health. About three acres in the centre were reserved as a children's playground. In 1917, during the food shortage caused by German U-boats at a critical point in the First World War, some of the Pleasure Ground was converted into thirty-two allotments.

Alphington Street in 1908 from near Exe Bridge, looking towards Alphington. The first shop on the right, 53, is the saddler, harness and collar maker owned by William Ridge Trickey. Next door at 52 is printer Harry Punchard and at 51, more visible on the card, is James Cornish Wills, a grocer and wine and spirit merchant. The sign further down the road is that of the Bullers Arms Inn, owned by Henry John Hart.

Alphington village in 1903. The central building is the old bakery, destroyed by fire in 1909 (See chapter 5). In the late eighteenth century, Charles Babbage was sent to a local school, run by a clergyman, who was instructed 'not to press too much knowledge on him'. In adult life he invented a calculating machine regarded now as the first computer! In 1839, Charles Dickens (a regular visitor to Exeter) rented a cottage in the village for his parents.

Saint David's Church, Hele Road in 1912. The foundation stone was laid on 28 July 1897, in the year of Queen Victoria's Diamond Jubilee and on the 1,300th anniversary of Saint Augustine's mission to the English. St David's replaced a church with an unusual tower, nicknamed the 'Pepper Pot', which had stood on the site since 1816. Praised for its architecture by Sir John Betjeman, it is one of only three Devon churches dedicated to the Welsh saint.

Saint David's station in 1907. When opened on 1 May 1844, two trains arrived: one from Bristol and Taunton, powered by two engines and crammed with 800 passengers, and the other from London, carrying Isambard Kingdom Brunel and numerous dignitaries. Initially comprising two buildings, in 1864 a new four-platform station was opened, which had an ornamental frontage and a massive partly-glazed roof. Between 1911 and 1914 the station was rebuilt.

EXWICK HILL
No 56B.

Above: Number 1 Exwick Hill in 1923. Thirty years earlier, in 1893, the corner had been rebuilt with the present striking black and white half timbering and a turret. By the time of this postcard it was a popular bakers and grocers owned by Mr H.H. Stile.

Left: Thatched cottages on Exwick Hill in 1908. At the top of this short section of the hill, the turning to the right is the square in which stands the Hermitage, a rambling thatched cottage with two wings, one of which probably dates from the sixteenth century. Samuel Banfill, one of the partners who established a woollen manufactory and fulling mills in Exwick in the eighteenth century, died here in 1843 aged eighty-one.

Sidwell Street in 1910. A busy street scene, as a horse-drawn coach stands outside
the White Lion Hotel, whose landlord was Arthur Lawless. On the right, a tram
passes the narrow entrance of Paris Street. At 6 (seen here on the left), Plimsoll
Clark and Company, grocers and provision merchants, claimed to be 'Providers for
the Million' in their Times Stores. On the extreme left of the postcard at 5 is a glass
and china shop owned by Mr Henry Avent.

Children wait to board one of the newly-introduced trams in Sidwell Street in 1905.
Three years earlier, French engineer Paul Cottalin, a pioneer in ferro-concrete, had
been selected to construct the new Wesleyan, now Methodist, church on the left,
but he went bankrupt during building, so now only the dome and gallery show
evidence of unusual construction. Past the church, 75 to 80 were demolished in
1937 when the Odeon cinema was built.

Whipton village in 1905, looking in the direction of Pinhoe. The name Whipton derives from a Saxon landowner called Wippa, who owned Wippa's farm. After the Norman invasion, Whipton, then called Wipletona was given to a wealthy landowner called William Capra. The manor covered 112 acres and was valued at £1 in the Domesday Book. Red sandstone from Whipton quarries was used in the building of Exeter Cathedral in 1341, and in the rebuilding of city churches in the fifteenth century.

Buttonholed patrons of the Whipton Inn prepare to leave on a charabanc outing in the 1920s. In 1927, the concertina-clutching man in the front could have been facing a £5 fine under one of the new 'Annoyances by Excursionists' by-laws introduced by the council, which prohibited the use of 'any noisy instrument', which was combined with 'any person or persons to make any loud singing or outcry while passing through the city to the annoyance of residents'.

Pinhoe village in 1905. In 1001, when Exeter was besieged by the Danes, a Saxon force of militia assembled at Pinhoe to relieve the town. In the resultant battle the Danes were victorious and the Saxons suffered heavy losses. The Danish force burned Pinhoe down, but were still unable to capture Exeter. In 1986 a national newspaper offered a year's lease on the thatched Heart of Oak pub, seen on the card, as a competition prize.

Pinhoe garage in the 1920s. Owned by ex-Royal Navy stoker Henry Bindon, survivor of three separate torpedo attacks, who after leaving his life at sea turned himself into a motor mechanic and owner of a highly successful filling station and repair garage. In his younger life he played football with Pinhoe AFC's cup-winning team.

Saint Michael's, the parish Church of Heavitree in 1905. The eminent historian W.G. Hoskins believed Heavitree to be the oldest christian site in the area outside Exeter, with a church probably built before the year 700. The twelfth-century church on the site was altered in the fourteenth and fifteenth centuries and entirely restored in 1541. A new limestone tower was added in 1887, designed by the diocesan surveyor Edward Harbottle to commemorate the Golden Jubilee of Queen Victoria.

The interior of Saint Michael's Church, Heavitree, *c.* 1910. In the fifteenth century, the nave, built of Heavitree stone, had six bays with richly carved angels, but by 1844 the stone had decayed and it was rebuilt, in a Gothic style, with limestone walls but retaining the old Beer stone arcade and windows. The architect was David Mackintosh. The interior was transformed in 1939 when the Cathedral reredos, shown on the next card, had been installed.

The Altar, Exeter Cathedral. Nº 11237.

The reredos in Exeter Cathedral in around 1915. Composed of alabaster and marble, enriched with gilding and a wealth of coloured gems, the decorative screen at the back of the altar was designed by Sir Gilbert Scott in 1870. In January 1874 it was the subject of a famous lawsuit initiated by Chancellor William John Philpotts, Archdeacon of Cornwall, son of a former Bishop of Exeter and a Prebendary of Exeter Cathedral. The archdeacon sought to prove that the carved representations of biblical scenes on the reredos were not 'sanctioned by the Laws Ecclesiastical' and had been erected without a faculty. Seeking to replace them with the Ten Commandments, Philpotts argued that they were idolatrous images. At the end of the case the bishop's assessor, Mr Justin Keating, found in favour of the plaintiff, ordering the dean and chapter to take down the reredos. However, on appeal, this decision was reversed and this verdict upheld by the Privy Council. If it had not been, all figure sculpture of whatever kind in any church would have become technically illegal. In May 1939, the interior core of the reredos was found to be defective and it was taken down and re-erected in Heavitree Parish Church later in the year.

The centre of the village of Countess Wear in 1930. The village takes its name from Isabella, the Countess of Devon who, in 1284, constructed two weirs to drive a mill near Topsham. Her successor Hugh de Courtenay, however, blocked the gap she left for shipping to pass to Exeter, forcing ships to offload at Topsham, greatly increasing his family fortunes. The city eventually built a canal to bypass the river.

Countess Wear Bridge in 1909. The new seven-arch bridge, built in 1774 by Mr Thomas Parker of Topsham, was the first to span the River Exe at Countess Wear. In 1842, two of the arches were converted into a single arch by Mr Robert Davy at a cost of £430, to allow his barges better passage through the bridge, especially when the river was flooded.

Right: Dutch houses in The Strand, Topsham in 1910. In the 1690s, when the Netherlands was the greatest customer for Devonshire serges, Dutch bricks came back to Topsham as ballast. Combined with the influence of personal contact between woollen merchants and their Dutch customers, it led to the building of a series of houses with Dutch-style gables between 1680 and 1730. The street is unique in the South West.

Below: Topsham pier in 1910. Built in 1887 to commemorate Queen Victoria's Golden Jubilee, it became a popular venue for summer Sunday concerts. By 1917, however, it had fallen into disrepair and when three boys attempted to jump a gap in its structure, one fell to his death. The pier was immediately closed and three years later dismantled.

The Pier, Topsham

Two horse-drawn carriages, the first led by Mr Frank Luxton, precede a horse-drawn manually operated fire engine and three firemen across the quay at Topsham, on 24 August 1907. The new engine was christened *Aphrodite* by local dignitary Mrs Ratcliff. Provision had been made for the 'accommodation of the parish fire-engine' by the Market House Trust in 1837.

Fire at Topsham on the afternoon of Thursday 19 August 1909. The sub-captain of the fire brigade, Mr H. Gould, dressed in a cape and cocked hat is seen directing firemen attempting to subdue a 'conflagration' in Passage Lane. Furniture from the burning thatched cottages was saved and the fire was prevented from reaching other buildings in the vicinity by the firemen, who were quickly in action, assisted by the local vicar and his curate. The nearby river provided a plentiful supply of water for the pumps.

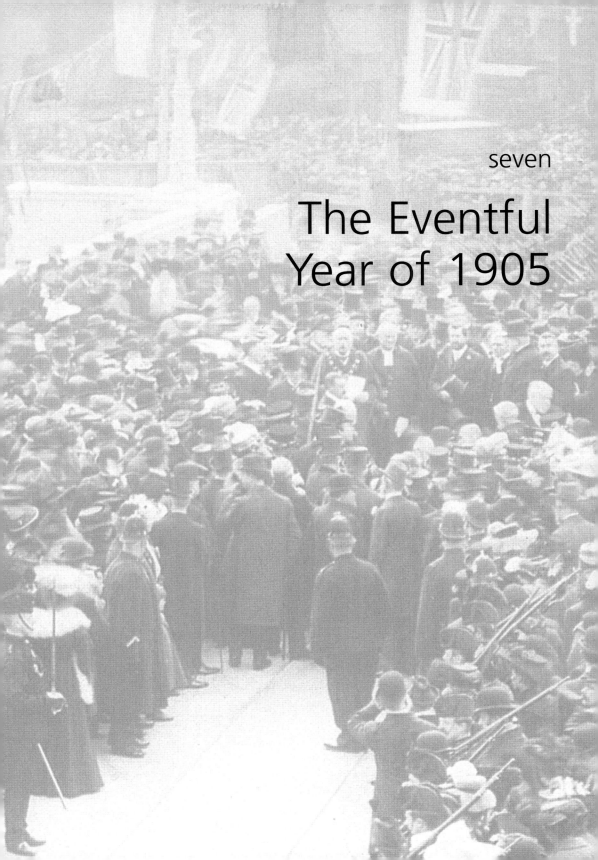

seven

The Eventful
Year of 1905

Old Exe Bridge in 1903. The three-arched bridge, built 'very handsomely of stone' in 1778 to replace a twelfth-century medieval bridge, had for many years posed problems for those who had to negotiate its gradient in slippery conditions. By the time of this postcard it was considered completely unsuitable for the proposed new electric tram service, which required a level crossing point over the river between Fore Street and Saint Thomas.

Dismantling Old Exe Bridge in December 1903. One year earlier, the first pile of a temporary wooden pontoon bridge was sunk to allow continued public access over the river. It was completed on 19 May. A week later the old bridge was closed and demolition began. The temporary wooden bridge can be seen behind the last remaining arch of the stone bridge.

Right: 'Exeter's Four Bridges': a card issued by *The Exeter Flying Post* in 1905. Costing one penny, the paper advertised the card as 'a little bit of history, with artistic illustrations of the Four Exe Bridges from the twelfth to the twentieth centuries'. The new steel bridge is shown as being complete in 1904 but it was not officially opened until 1905.

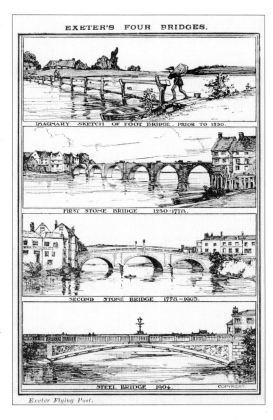

Below: A souvenir postcard of 1904 showing the first stages of construction of the new bridge. Concrete laying for the new bridge began on the Saint Thomas side of the river on 29 October 1903, and the corner foundation stone was laid on 23 July 1904. The cost of construction was £26,000, and the bridge was designed by Sir John Wolfe Barry and Mr C.A. Brereton.

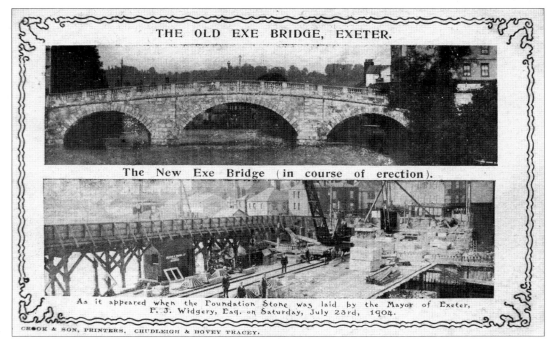

The opening of Exe Bridge on 29 March 1905. At noon on a day of dull weather, thousands of Exonians, eager to see the first event of a momentous year in the city's history, surrounded the bridge, which was adorned with strings of flags. A barricade had been erected at each end of the bridge and admission to the bridge itself was by ticket. A hundred-strong guard of honour from the Rifle Volunteers, under Captain Parsons, was present with the battalion band. Order was kept by twenty-seven members of the city police, two of whom were mounted, reinforced by twenty-five county constables. Opening the bridge by cutting a cord suspended from poles on either side, the mayor, Councillor Edwin C. Perry, included in his speech a welcome to Sir Redvers Buller, who was among the many dignitaries present. When the procession from the bridge was passing through the barrier on their way to lunch at the Guildhall, a large section of the crowd outside attempted to rush on to the bridge, but the police and the military prevented a possibly serious incident.

Thousands of Exonians, kept back by barriers and police while the official speeches were made, flood on to the 150ft long new bridge on 29 March 1905. So enthusiastic were the crowds that Fore Street, Alphington Street, Cowick Street and Alphington Road were completely blocked by people waiting to cross the bridge. Onlookers also clung to rooftops eager to witness the historic scene.

The new bridge had been built and officially opened but, later in 1905, the temporary wooden pontoon bridge was still in position and can be seen under the arch. On 8 July the tablets, which revealed the past history of the previous bridges and the commemoration of the new one, were quietly removed, revealed as being only temporary plates and replaced by the finished real bronze ones – three months after the event!

Hundreds of people awaiting the second major event of the year: the arrival of the first electrically powered trams in Exeter, near Eastgate, on 4 April 1905. The new trams were 26ft long and weighed eight and a half tons. Painted green with gold and yellow lines, they were decorated for the occasion with red, green or blue, combined with white drapery.

The mayor, Councillor Edwin C. Perry, addressing a large crowd outside the Guildhall on 4 April 1905. Standing on the top deck of the first of a line of five cars, he said that by the inauguration of its splendidly equipped electrical tramway service, Exeter had placed itself 'in the van of progress' and had brought itself into line with the principal cities and towns of the United Kingdom.

The mayor drives one of the first trams on 4 April 1905. It was decorated with festoons of ivy, laurel and daffodils, bunches of primroses and palms and flags of red and yellow, the colours of the city. At three o'clock, Exonians filled the new trams as the service was opened to the public, 7,740 people travelling on the first day for twopence each. By 8 July the number of passengers carried had reached one million.

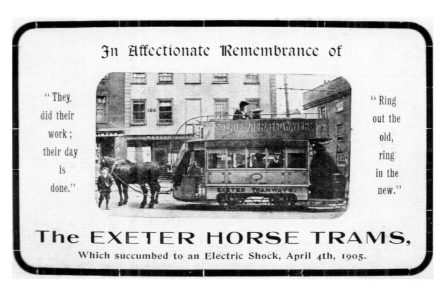

In Affectionate Remembrance of

"They did their work; their day is done."

"Ring out the old, ring in the new."

The EXETER HORSE TRAMS,
Which succumbed to an Electric Shock, April 4th, 1905.

The last of the horse-drawn trams in Sidwell Street in March 1905. On 22 March it was announced that the council was to arrange for the disposal of the horses that had operated the system. Twenty-two were subsequently auctioned on 7 April for a total of £263 11s 6d. One of those purchased fell, receiving fatal injuries, while only 200 yards from the sale. The purchaser was awarded half the cost of the horse in compensation. The trams were auctioned on 26 June for between £4 and £6 each.

Mayor Tom Linscott drives the first tram over Exe Bridge, on its way to the Stone Lane terminus, to open the Alphington Road extension on Tuesday 18 September 1906. At five o'clock the mayor, accompanied by members of the corporation and officials, had boarded the two decorated cars at the Guildhall. The party included Edwin Perry, chairman of the Tramways Committee, who as mayor had opened the tram service the previous year. He is seen in a dark suit holding onto an upright alongside the driver. The new section of the tram system was constructed by Messrs Ireland of Morecambe. Behind the vast crowds on the Saint Thomas end of the new Exe Bridge is the shop of the well-known Exeter seed merchant Samuel Randall, which opened on this site in 1880. In February 1905, Mr Randall complained to the council that while the bridge was being built his shop had been completely cut off from the main thoroughfare by hoardings, resulting in a considerable loss of trade. The council denied legal liability but awarded Mr Randall an ex gratia payment of £100. Damaged during the Blitz, the shop was subsequently demolished.

Right: General Sir Redvers Henry Buller and Lady Audrey Jane Charlotte Buller in 1904. Born at Downes, Crediton in 1839, Redvers Buller had an outstanding army career. Commissioned at eighteen, he served in China and South Africa, where, in the Zulu War of 1878-9 as a colonel, he won the Victoria Cross. In 1882 he received the KCMG and was appointed chief of staff for the relief of Khartoum in 1884. General Buller was in command of British forces in the first Boer War and relieved Ladysmith with Lord Roberts in 1900. He married Lady Audrey, daughter of the 4th Marquis Townshend, in 1882. During the South African War and First World War, she worked tirelessly for the sick and wounded, as did their only daughter, Audrey Charlotte Georgiana, whose name was usually shortened to Georgiana, during the First World War.

Gen. Sir Redvers and Lady Audrey Buller

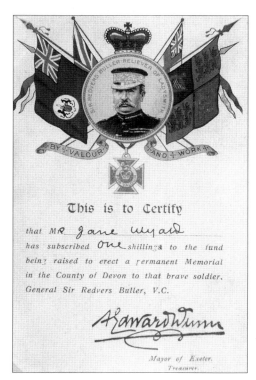

SIR·REDVERS·BULLER·RELIEVER·OF·LADY·S·TH

BY · VALOUR · AND · WORK

This is to Certify

that MR *Jane Wyard*

has subscribed *One* shillings to the fund being raised to erect a permanent Memorial in the County of Devon to that brave soldier, General Sir Redvers Buller, V.C.

Edward Wynn

Mayor of Exeter.
Treasurer.

Left: A special postcard sent in 1901 to thank Mrs Jane Wyard for her contribution of one shilling towards the funding of a statue to commemorate General Buller. She was one of 50,000 subscribers to the fund, in Britain and overseas, which had been launched that October.

Unveiling of S...
Exeter Septe...

Top-hatted chairmen of district councils in Devon, Cornwall and Somerset, followed by the mayor and councillors in full regalia, and other dignitaries, near the statue of General Redvers Buller on 6 September 1905. The procession had left the Guildhall at 12.45 p.m. and was due at the statue at 1 p.m. All traffic had been stopped in High Street, in Queen Street and in every side street. The 1st Rifle Volunteers provided the guard of honour. By now the morning rain had cleared and the sunshine was 'bright and scorching' as the Cathedral bells rang in the distance, in 'tribute to a friend'. On the streets, among the thousands of Exonians and visitors, vendors sold postcards and other mementoes of the occasion, including handkerchiefs printed with a timetable of the days events, a picture of the statue, and a list of the general's medals.

Above: The statue cloaked in the White Ensign before the unveiling and commemoration ceremony at 1 p.m. on 6 September 1905. The bronze statue, which weighed four tons and stood on a 10ft 8in pedestal of Cornish granite, had been guarded for a month before the ceremony. Afterwards the chief constable was instructed to protect it from boys loitering in the vicinity, who might have thrown stones at it!

Right: The statue of General Sir Redvers Buller stands proudly on its plinth with the mayor standing beneath on the raised platform surrounding it, on 6 September 1905. Speaking at the last of the three major events of his momentous mayoralty, Councillor Edwin Perry said that the statue was a magnificent gift to the city of Exeter, and also 'a magnificent work of art'.

The vast crowd gathers round General Buller's statue on 6 September 1905. The unveiling was performed by the Lord Lieutenant of Devon, Viscount Ebrington, who had stood in for Lord Wolseley, an old friend of the general, absent through illness. Using Lord Wolseley's notes, the Viscount said 'This statue will remind future generations of Western men of the brilliant services performed by Devon's most illustrious son of this period'. On pulling the cord which released the flag, the Exeter Oratorio Society and the Male Voice Choir sang *Land of Hope and Glory*.

As well as the many invited guests, tickets were available to others at 2s 6d in the grandstand fronting the statue, 1s in the reserved enclosure at the Hele Road entrance and 6d at the Queen Street entrance. Police were paid extra for their special duty. The event was followed by a reception and luncheon at the Victoria Hall, at which Sir Redvers and Lady Buller and their daughter Georgiana were the special guests. At five o'clock a tea was given at Bury Meadow to army and navy veterans, many of whom had served with General Buller. The ceremony closed with the playing of the National Anthem by the band of the 4th Battalion King's Royal Rifles. When Sir Redvers was seen by the 'great crowd' he was 'greeted with tremendous cheers'.

Right: The statue of General Buller draped in black after his death at 12.40 a.m. on 2 June 1908. At Crediton, a procession of more than 2,000 people, including many military personnel, accompanied the coffin on its way to the Churchyard. The committal sentences were read by the Bishop of Exeter and, as the coffin was lowered into its last resting place, twenty buglers from the King's Royal Rifles sounded the Last Post, accompanied by a salute from seventeen guns of the Royal Field Artillery.

Below: An advertising card for the Fifth Annual Trades Exhibition, held at the Victoria Hall from 4 to 14 April 1905. Replicas of Exeter's ancient streets and buildings, including the Guildhall, Mol's Coffee House and the Castle filled the hall, which was lit by electric lighting, then the new technology. Within the replicas were twenty-seven trade stands, many with innovative exhibits, including a forerunner of strip lighting – the 'linolite' – and the latest vacuum cleaners as well as more traditional exhibits such as pianos, pictures and pottery. Music was 'supplied by an orchestra of lady harpists'.

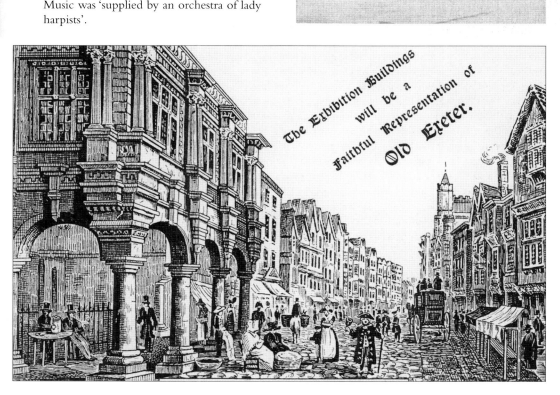

The Exhibition Buildings will be a Faithful Representation of Old Exeter.

Other local titles published by Tempus

Dartmoor
TOM GREEVES

The rich history of Dartmoor can be seen in the 200 archive photographs and postcards in this book. The images recall life as it once was on Dartmoor: the towns, villages and local people who lived and worked on the moor between the 1860s and the 1950s. From farming and mining to social gatherings such as hunts, races and fairs, each picture records the everyday life of these resilient communities.

0 7524 3146 3

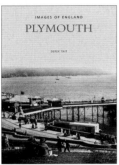

Plymouth
DEREK TAIT

Plymouth has seen many changes over the years and this collection of over 200 archive photographs and postcards features many images of a pre-war Plymouth now long gone. There are nostalgic glimpses of the old pier, Plymouth Hoe and the grand old theatres, where Harry Houdini and Laurel and Hardy were among the performers. This book is sure to bring back memories for all who know and love this city.

0 7524 3128 5

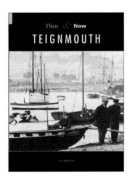

Teignmouth Then & Now
VIV WILSON

Teignmouth has seen many changes during its long history as a port, a fishing and boat-building town and a holiday resort. This book illustrates some of the changes that have occurred over the last hundred years by comparing a series of old photographs with modern ones taken from exactly the same locations. The reader can follow the changes and then revisit the locations to see them in a new light.

0 7524 3368 7

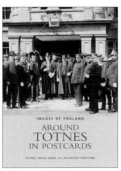

Around Totnes in Postcards
TOTNES IMAGE BANK AND ROSEMARY DENSHAM

This selection of 180 postcards from the Totnes Image Bank collection illustrates the bustling history of this town and the surrounding area, including Dartington, Ipplepen and Ashprington. The ancient castle and Elizabethan buildings are featured and events such as carnivals, Empire Day celebrations and the relocation of the Victoria Memorial Fountain are recalled. The images will evoke memories for some and provide a fascinating glimpse of the past for others.

0 7524 3190 0

If you are interested in purchasing other books published by Tempus, or in case you have difficulty finding any Tempus books in your local bookshop, you can also place orders directly through our website

www.tempus-publishing.com